BRINGING PROGRESS
to PARADISE

D1052529

BRINGING PROGRESS
to PARADISE

What I Got from Giving to a Mountain Village in Nepal

Jeff Rasley

Conari Press

First published in 2010 by
Red Wheel/Weiser, LLC
With offices at:
500 Third Street, Suite 230
San Francisco, CA 94107
www.redwheelweiser.com

Copyright © 2010 by Jeff Rasley
All rights reserved. No part of this publication may be reproduced or
transmitted in any form or by any means, electronic or mechanical,
including photocopying, recording, or by any information storage and
retrieval system, without permission in writing from Red Wheel/Weiser,
LLC. Reviewers may quote brief passages.

Some names are changed to protect privacy.
Additional photographs of Basa village and other Himalayan
expeditions may be viewed at the author's website: *www.jeffreyrasley.com.*

ISBN: 978-1-57324-482-4

Library of Congress Cataloging-in-Publication Data available upon
request.

Cover design: Stewart Williams
Text design: Donna Linden
Typeset in Goudy Oldstyle and Perpetua
Cover photograph © Richard Kischuk

Printed in Canada
TCP
10 9 8 7 6 5 4 3 2 1

Dedicated to Alicia who is my home;
and to my friends and sirdars
Niru Rai, Ganesh Rai, and Sanga Rai;
and to the three lost on Zatwra La;
and to Basa village.

ACKNOWLEDGMENTS

Ang Nima Sherpa, my first sirdar; John Roskelley and Tom Proctor, who taught me mountaineering; K P Kafle, Hari Pudasaini, and Seth Chetri, who helped open my eyes to the beauty of Nepal; Uttam Phuyal, my friend and Katmandu caretaker; Sheila Candler, my loyal assistant; Dave Wood, my former partner and clothier; all my trekking and mountaineering companions from 1995 through 2009; the donors to the Basa School Project for their generosity; J J and Kate for their technical assistance; Caroline Pincus, my sensitive editor; my sons James and Andrew; and my parents, who gave me life and love.

CONTENTS

⬚ ⬚ ◉ ◉ ⬚ ◉ ◉ ⬚ ◉

Ama Dablam mountain from Khumjung village in the Khumbu

PROLOGUE

We were five ghostly figures in swirling snow, standing atop the 15,000-foot Zatwra La. Early morning rays of sun crept over and down the flank of the great white peak behind us. Wind blowing from the north made it hard to hear the others. Heather shouted over the hushing wind, "We've got to spread out!" But Tom insisted we should stay close together. All our rope was with our porters, who were slogging up the pass an hour or so behind us. Suddenly, Heather yelped and took off running. Tom cursed. Seth bellowed, "Go, run!" And then I heard the low distant roar that mountain climbers dread.

We took off down the pass with Heather in the lead. Judy cried out and fell down. Tom and Seth grabbed her arms, pulling her up, yelling at her, "Run! Run!"

I saw them out of the corner of my eye as I pounded mechanically down the rocky, snow-covered slope, stumbling into and over boulders hidden by snow. My consciousness was a gray crackling static. I knew my ability to think and respond was impaired by altitude sickness. All I felt was an instinctive drive to keep running, to get off this mountain, to survive.

The roar of the avalanche above and behind us was replaced by an eerie whirring sound. Spindrift came over us, stark white and opaque. I could barely see my gloves and boots. But the avalanche had petered out. We fell to our knees gasping. We looked up into a vast whiteness.

The avalanche struck when our team was hiking out from base camp after a failed attempt to climb 21,224-foot Mera Peak in the fall of 1999 in the Solu-Khumbu region of Nepal. Fifteen climbing teams spent most of the first week of October stuck in base camp or high camp. With unrelenting snow and terrible visibility, conditions were too tough to make a summit attempt. During my team's eleven-day trek to the Mera base camp at 16,000 feet, we were rained on every day until we got above 14,000 feet. From then on, it snowed every day.

The trek was surrealistic, over high mountain passes, across rushing glacier-fed streams. We slipped and slid through a muddy bamboo forest and past the remains of a village destroyed the year before by an avalanche. Everything—our gear, boots, clothes—was soaking wet by the time we got above the rain, camping then in snow and ice. Our progress was slowed after that by having to slog through deep snow. After four days enduring heavy snows and blizzard conditions in base camp and high camp, our team gave up. I spent the last day on the mountain in a tent by myself, retching and wretched with altitude sickness and a sinus infection.

Snow continued to fall as our defeated and bedraggled team finally hiked out of base camp. At sunrise on the second day of the hike out, our tents sagged under five inches of new snow that had fallen during the night. Snow continued falling as we ate breakfast, packed gear, and then trudged 2,000 feet up the backside of the 15,000-foot pass called Zatrwa La. This was the last high pass to cross to escape the menace of avalanche from the great white-capped Himalayan peaks and to reach Lukla village, where a Twin Otter airplane was scheduled to fly us back to Katmandu. By the time we postholed up to the crest of the pass, fresh snow was over two feet deep. The conditions were perfect for an avalanche: fresh, deep, and unstable snow.

Barely visible through the falling snow on a ridge above and behind us were splotches of red and yellow—the down parkas of three Nepalese porters from another climbing expedition that was following us out of the mountains. The three Nepalese guys were inching their way across the ridge, slowed by the blowing snow and the heavy loads they were carrying.

When the avalanche struck, my team was on the crest of the Zatwra La trying to decide how to descend the steep 4,000-foot slope. The avalanche came down off a mountain shoulder well above and behind us, but right above the three Nepalese porters. They vanished in the gigantic wave of the avalanche. It wasn't until we were safely back in Lukla village that we learned the porters had been killed, along with four others who died in a series of avalanches across the Nepal-Tibetan Himalaya that same week of October 1999.

Of those seven deaths, only one garnered international headlines, that of the famous mountaineer Alex Lowe on Shishapangma in Tibet. If the deaths of six Nepalese porters in the avalanches were noted at all, it was as a footnote to the loss of a great Western mountaineer.

The three porters I saw enveloped in the death grip of the avalanche were known to me only as workers for another climbing expedition of Western adventurers. They lost their lives carrying heavy loads while taking a higher, harder shortcut out of base camp to get their employers' gear to Lukla before the climbers arrived.

⬚ ⬛ ◉ ◌ ▣

The arc of this story begins with three being enveloped in an avalanche of death and ends in three being enveloped in an avalanche of love in a village called Basa. After that avalanche in 1999 I did not expect to return to Nepal. But Nepal had a hold on me and would not let go. Why did I feel such a strong pull to return even after the awfulness of the failed expedition to Mera Peak? It took almost ten years for me to fully answer the question.

I first went to the Himalayas out of curiosity and returned several times as an adventurer. However, since 2003, I have returned almost every year to try and give back to a country that has given much to me. My purpose has not been to alleviate poverty. Poverty is a relative term, and lack of material wealth by American standards is not in itself a misfortune. What I have tried to do since 2003 is to respond to specific requests for assistance from Nepalese friends who work in remote mountain villages by helping to create mutually beneficial relationships with friends in the West.

Our modern consumer culture has turned human beings into tools of commerce. Adam Smith and Karl Marx both agreed that modern human identity is determined by the value of one's labor. We are what we do. ("Hi, my name is Jeff. I'm a lawyer. What do you do?") But our work separates us from nature and our essential nature as humans. Nature is to be exploited for consumption by the market, to be used up. We tear up the earth digging for coal and pollute the land and water drilling for oil. People are objectified as "the market." Human beings have become a sort of malleable matter, the purpose of which is to consume and produce.

But people who live close to the earth in tune with nature's rhythms are in cooperation with the land and its bounty. The earth and its resources are not to be used up but to be continuously recycled. Yak dung becomes fuel. A yak becomes clothing and food, but not before another is born to take its place. The land is tilled according to the eternal cycle of the seasons. Neighbors are not separated by security systems but are "our people." We are a clan, a tribe; we are Sherpa or Rai.

A village called Basa in the land of the Rai gave me the answer to my question of 1999 about why I should keep coming back to Nepal. The Rai believe that everything, whether animate or inanimate, has spirit and deserves respect. We modern Westerners long for a more soulful way of life. That is why stories such as that told in James Cameron's film *Avatar* are so compelling. We identify with the poor "primitives" instead of the rich "civilized." We long to live closer to nature and to be more essentially human in our relations. People who have lived the same way for centuries, without wheels, electricity, or plumbing, welcomed two friends and me into the village of Basa. They welcomed us with an avalanche of love.

But now the question has become: What can we give to Basa that it really needs, and can we give to Basa without destroying it by allowing it to become too much like us?

PTSD

I turned forty in 1993 and began manifesting symptoms of a midlife crisis. I whined about the responsibilities of marriage, two kids, a law business, and a mortgage. All the responsibilities and obligations were sucking the life out of me. Buying a Harley didn't cure it.

One evening my wife slapped a brochure down on the coffee table in front of me and said in a steely tone, "Why don't you do this? Go climb a mountain." The brochure advertised a Himalayan trekking expedition. I'd lived at sea level in Indiana most of my life and had no trekking or climbing experience. But I had done a lot of rugged outdoor activities, so I was intrigued. Alicia may later have regretted her "go take a hike" therapy, because I fell in love—with the mountains.

My friend and chiropractor, Long John, and I went trekking along the Everest Base Camp trail in Sagarmatha Park, Nepal, in the spring of 1995 in a five-member group through an American expedition company called Snow Lion. The group had an American guide but was really led by a sirdar (chief trekking guide) named Ang Nima Sherpa, and it was staffed by Nepalese mountain dwellers. I had never met anyone as strong, kind, and admirable as Nima, and the spectacular beauty of the Himalayas turned me on like no other place in the more than thirty countries I had visited in my travels.

Adventure travel was part of my life before travel companies packaged it in brochures. As a teenager I hitchhiked across the United States and traveled around Europe on buses and trains. In my twenties and thirties, I motorcycled around Mexico, scuba dived throughout the Caribbean, went horseback riding and four-wheeling in Belize, and kayaked around islands in the South Pacific and the Ionian Sea. From each of these experiences, I was enriched through encounters with different lands, cultures, and people. But my encounter with the Himalayan mountains and Nepalese-Tibetan culture on that introductory trek in 1995 touched me so deeply I could hardly wait to return.

During the next two summers, I took introductory and intermediate climbing courses at Seneca Rock, West Virginia. I joined my first mountaineering expedition to Ladakh, India, in 1996, led by the renowned American climber and writer John Roskelley. I went back to Nepal on increasingly challenging expeditions in 1998 and 1999. I didn't climb 8,000-meter (25,000 foot) peaks or attempt extreme climbs requiring oxygen tanks and hanging off sheer walls in bivy bags. As a father, husband, and attorney with staff and family to support, I knew becoming a climber bum wasn't in the cards; and I'm far too cheap to spend $65,000 and six weeks to attempt Mount Everest. Trekking for a couple of weeks and climbing 20,000-foot peaks was sufficiently challenging and wonderful for me.

For a middle-aged Hoosier flatlander, Himalayan mountaineering and trekking is difficult in terms of the conditioning required and the physical and emotional stress of a long trek followed by twelve to twenty-four hours of climbing. It's grueling, and when weather conditions are bad, it's dangerous. But I loved it. The Himalayas pulled me back each year. That is, until the disastrous expedition to Mera. The experience of advanced acute mountain sickness, barely escaping an avalanche, and seeing three porters disappear broke the mountains' grip on me.

Off the Mountaintop

Six months after my return from the Mera Peak expedition, I was driving home from my office in downtown Indianapolis. Without warning, tears started streaming down my face, and I had to pull over to the side of the street. I sat in the car and cried. I could no longer hold in the feelings of guilt and shame. The picture of the three porters just before they were enveloped in the tsunami of white snow was seared in my mind. I had done nothing to try to help. I could do nothing to help. But the memory wouldn't release me.

The author of Ecclesiastes (1.14–15) wrote, "All is futile and a striving after wind. What is crooked cannot be made straight." I found myself overwhelmed with existential despair, feeling the unfairness of life and the futility of trying to do anything about it. It was unfair and awful that the lives of those three hardworking men could be snuffed out in an instant. I had no more thirst for adventures in the Himalayas; my throat was dry.

I had participated in four Himalayan expeditions in five years. But after the avalanche, I did not return to Nepal for four years. It was no longer safe to visit anyway. SARS had broken out in Asia, and Nepal was undergoing a violent Maoist revolution against the king. The army was shooting demonstrators in the streets of Katmandu, and Maoists were blowing up buildings and bombing buses. In a shocking incident in June 2001, Crown Prince Dipendra shot and killed his parents and siblings as they sat down to dinner, and then shot himself. Political instability followed, because many Nepalese distrusted the new king, Gyanendra, brother to the murdered Birendra. Some even suspected that Gyanendra was involved in the murders. Nepal was put on the U.S. State Department's travel warning list. Then came 9/11.

The allure of Nepal as a magical kingdom for Western adventurers was lost. In 1999, more than 500,000 tourists visited Nepal. By 2002, less than half that number entered the kingdom.

Religious people equate a "mountaintop experience" with a spiritual awakening or a transcendent connection with God. Why equate being on top of a mountain with experiencing God? Because feeling the awesomeness of the natural world on top of a mountain is such a glorious feeling that the limitations of language force us to call it "God." Every day of a mountaineering expedition or high-altitude trek, that feeling is available.

John Muir described "the ecstasy of the surrender to nature." He meant that by opening oneself to natural beauty, the soul is magnified to a point of transcendence beyond the ordinary consciousness of task-oriented living. During each of my Himalayan expeditions, I surrendered to the ecstasy of nature. I learned and lived what John Muir described.

But after the disaster of the 1999 Mera Peak expedition and what followed, I'd had enough. The dark side of nature then got a hold of me. I was sick of being tired, cold, and sick. To hell with the Himalayas. I was done with mountains. So I went kayaking and diving in sunny Palau, a remote archipelago near Micronesia.

2

JUBILEE

May 29, 2003 was the Golden Jubilee of the first recorded summit of Mount Everest by Tenzing Norgay and Sir Edmund Hillary on that date in 1953. That first summit of Everest, the highest mountain on planet Earth, turned the world's attention to the Kingdom of Nepal.

Nepal's economy badly needed tourists to return. The Maoists and the government, at war with each other, declared a truce for the Jubilee. Sir Edmund Hillary's family put its considerable resources to work at bringing tourists back to Nepal for the Jubilee celebrations. Sir Edmund would cohost with the King of Nepal a black-tie affair in Katmandu. Hillary's son, Peter, would cohost with the Rinpoche Tenzing, the Incarnate Lama of Tengboche Monastery, the "highest party in the world" on the monastery grounds at 12,700 feet. Mountaineers around the world were invited to return for the celebrations.

I was born in 1953, just a month before the first summit of Mount Everest. It had been almost ten years since my first trek along the Base Camp Trail. As the Jubilee approached, the magnetism of Nepal pulled me back.

The last three weeks of May 2003, I trekked with my friend and translator Hari Pudasaini through Sagarmatha National Park in the Khumbu region of Nepal along the Everest Base Camp Trail up to base camp at 18,000 feet. Along the trail, I interviewed many Sherpas and mountaineers to do research for an article about the celebrations and the effect of tourism on Sherpa culture. Members of the Hillary family were making a pilgrimage along the Base Camp Trail, which became the most famous hiking trail in the world after Hillary and Norgay hiked it on their way to Mount Everest in 1953. The Hillary clan stopped at the Hillary School in Khumjung, the first of several schools built by Hillary's foundation, the Himalayan Trust, and inspected Kunde Hospital, the first medical clinic established by the trust.

After Sir Edmund Hillary became rich and world-famous, he devoted much of the rest of his life to philanthropy for the Sherpa people. He greatly admired the unique character of strength and Buddhist gentleness he found in the high mountain people of Nepal. The assistance of Sherpas employed by his climbing team led to him becoming one of the most famous people of the 20th century, and he gratefully returned many times to the Khumbu, home to the Sherpas. His philanthropic efforts brought schools, medical clinics, and eventually hydroelectric projects to the Sherpas. And the Sherpas loved him back. They called him "King of the Khumbu."

The Two Sides of Tourism

I hiked to Phakding with Sir Edmund's older sister, June, who was then 86. During dinner, the intrepid octogenarian reminisced, "When Ed was young, he loved to personally work on laying brick and stone to help build schools and medical clinics in Sherpa villages. He had so much fun!" But not all of the dinner talk was so sanguine about the last fifty years for the Sherpas of the Khumbu. In response to my question about how the Sherpas had been affected by tourism, a grandniece of Hillary exclaimed, "It's bad!" She argued that the renowned toughness of the Sherpas had been softened by material gain from tourism, and the Buddhist gentleness had been hardened by the pursuit of money. At breakfast the next morning, Hillary Carlyle, June's daughter, confessed, "It's hard for us to judge whether the Western influence and tourism has been good for the Sherpas. My uncle has been such a significant part of all that." She told me she'd been to the Khumbu five or six times, "but it seems like I'm always here—it's the family business, you know."

The enthusiasm of the Hillary family for helping to better the lives of Sherpas was inspiring, but I was conflicted about the overall impact we Westerners have had on Sherpa culture. The Western influence can be seen in the villages along the trails that have become popular with trekkers and climbers in the Himalayas, especially the Everest Base Camp Trail. The lives of the villagers changed dramatically in the fifty years following Hillary's "conquering" of Chomolungma (the name of Mount Everest in the Tibetan language). Tourism in the Khumbu has affected Sherpa culture by turning many Sherpas from yak herders to lodge owners, or to guides, cooks, or porters working for expeditions. Tourism has brought trash and garbage into the majestic peaks and valleys of the Khumbu. Before the climbers and trekkers came, there was no metal, paper, or plastic in the Khumbu. Everything the Sherpas used was recyclable, because they had no man-made or manufactured products. Everything they made or used came from the yak, earth, or plants: clothes from yak hide and fuel from yak shit; shelter from stone and wood; and food grown in plots of rice, barley, corn, and potatoes. The mountaineers and trekkers brought packaged products and trash along the Base Camp Trail. The trail has become a potpourri of international litter—tobacco packs from India, beer bottles from Spain, blown-out boots from China, and ripped t-shirts from the United States.

Yet Mahendra Kathet, the headmaster at the Hillary school in Khumjung, told me in 2003, "Without tourism, we couldn't survive here." He has taught at the school since 1976. He flatly stated that no one in Khumjung thinks the changes brought about by tourism have been bad for the village. "Even the old people who maintain traditional dress think changes are good, because they have better food, like salt. Life is much easier." He related that before the Himalayan Trust built the school in 1961, people in Khumjung lived at a subsistence level. A guide employed by Peter Hillary's company, Ang Temba Sherpa, put it simply, "If you had the choice between walking two hours downhill and then back uphill carrying a bucket of water for the day, or having water piped to your house, which would you choose?"

The Highest Party in the World

Lama Tenzing is a small slight man with white hair. His skin is a soft mahogany. He wears a mango-colored cloak. He is revered by Sherpa Buddhists as a lama and the abbot of Tengboche Monastery. Lama Tenzing receives visitors every day and considers welcoming visitors one of his most important duties. He sits placidly on his divan looking at his guests with kindly interested eyes. His facial expression rarely changes. Decorating the wall behind him are brightly colored thangka paintings (sacred Buddhist paintings on cloth) draped with lengths of red silk.

A few days before the "highest party in the world" took place on the grounds of the monastery, Hari and I shared tea with Lama Tenzing. When I asked him what he thought of the effect of tourism on Sherpa culture, he responded through Hari's translation that he was "not happy and not upset about Western influence on Sherpas. People should do what they want."

As I walked across the grounds of the monastery back to the lodge where Hari and I were staying, cumulus clouds to the north cleared and the Everest Massif emerged in its spectacular majesty. A single cirrus cloud trailed like a kite tail from the pinnacle of the highest peak on Earth. The sound of monks chanting in the monastery echoed across the valley. I was looking at perfection. The aesthetic bliss of the Himalayas and Buddhist chanting was working its magic on me.

Bringing Progress to Paradise

Lama Tenzing

Tengboche Monastery

Pilgrims from all over the world endure the strenuous trek to Tengboche to be rewarded with this experience. Peace and harmony emanate from this beautiful human creation, developed by the ethics and aesthetics of Tibetan Buddhism and refined over a history of 2,500 years. Surrounded by the most magnificent natural scenery in the world, visitors apprehend the resident monks' harmonious discipline and are invited by the Incarnate Lama to participate in the peaceful character of the community.

But the night of the Jubilee party, the character of the monastery changed.

The official party commenced in a big blue tent erected on the monastery grounds at 4:00 p.m. There were many speeches, a fine dinner of yak steak and champagne, and black bowties for male attendees. Ladies wore long evening dresses over hiking boots. Peter Hillary, Sir Edmund's son, served as master of ceremonies. I know this not because I was inside the tent, but because I was outside looking in. About a hundred of us uninvited guests who had not paid $400 for an official invitation stood outside the tent for over an hour trying to eyeball and listen to the festivities inside. Employees of Hillary's trekking company were stationed around the tent, and a particularly burly fellow stood at the entrance with a lethal-looking two-foot-long club in his hand. Sherpa hospitality was not the order of the day for the official celebration at Tengboche.

Eventually, most of us impecunious voyeurs drifted into the meal room in the nearby Gompa Lodge. Pints of Mount Everest Whisky, a quite nasty drink brewed in Lukla, appeared. The manager, who wore monkish garb, brought out a cassette player and blasted techno music at full volume from the little recorder. A few porters entertained the crowd with a Nepalese version of techno dancing. We clapped and hooted for the dancers and passed the pints around.

After an hour or two, someone burst in and shouted that the tent was open. Everyone dashed out of the lodge and into the big blue tent. Two porters began to thump out a beat on gourd drums as others chanted the erotic lyrics of a Nepalese folk song. The crowd began to clap and sway to the beat of the drums. The rhythmic beat, clapping, and singing got more frenetic. Women were hoisted onto men's shoulders as Nepalis of all ethnic groups and trekkers and climbers from all over the world shouted and clapped to the pounding beat. Loose-limbed Nepalis, longhaired trekker girls, scruffy sunburnt mountain climbers, and spiritual seeking trekkers got down and the dancing got wilder.

At 10:30 p.m., the lights in the tent were extinguished. But the spirit of revelry propelled the crowd into a snake dance out of the tent and across the monastery grounds to the porter dormitory. A huge bonfire was lit and flames and ashes shot up into the night sky. Dancing, drumming, and singing around the fire went on till after midnight. Then, fifty or so remaining revelers danced back across the grounds and behind the monastery to the edge of an overlook above a 500-foot drop. We danced and sang for another hour, shining our headlamps in a communal beacon up at the stars.

The joy of a Bacchanalia is the loss of individuation, the letting go of self, not the loss of consciousness, but the loss of self-consciousness. We had clapped and stomped our feet and swayed to the rhythm of the drums. People from different parts of the world, who had never met before, grabbed each other and danced. We were liberated, in the words of the Rinpoche, "to do what we wanted."

Magnetic Effect of Nepal

The Jubilee experience had a magnetic effect on me. I felt the pull of Nepal again, but it was more than the mountains, the culture, and the need for adventure. My encounters with Sir Edmund Hillary's family and my interviews of Sherpas compelled me to think about what I could do for Nepal and then to act. I did not want to stew in my ambivalence about the impact of Western consumerism on Himalayan villagers. I'm not rich or famous, like Sir Edmund, and I don't have the time or inclination to own and operate an expedition company, like Peter Hillary. But I do have friends, and so I thought I could help to make a positive connection between Nepal and friends from the West.

I decided I would organize expeditions and contract directly with Nepalese expedition companies. All of the economic benefit from the expedition would thus go to local people. One of the most expensive components of a Western guiding company's charges is the cost of the Western guide—his wages, his transport to and from Nepal, and his living expenses. By not paying an American or European guide, I would be able to introduce friends to Nepal at a lower cost, with all of the wages going to Nepalese staff. Organizing fundraising projects was also part of the plan, and I hoped the friends who would experience Nepal through the expeditions would want to support projects to benefit mountain villages.

I began implementing the plan in October 2004 with an expedition of three: my old buddy Elliot from University of Chicago Rugby Club days; Briggie, a South African woman Elliot and I met in Katmandu; and me. I raised and delivered $1,000 for a village water project in Dolpo, a remote and poor area in western Nepal, and brought sixty-five pounds of school supplies to be distributed by a non-governmental agency run by my Nepalese friend, K. P. Kafle. In 2006, seven friends joined the expedition I organized to Gokyo, Lobuche, and Tengboche. In 2007, nine came with me, five from the Central Indiana Wilderness Club, and we handed out school supplies and gave stuffed animals to children along the trails we hiked in Helambu and Langtang. Several members of those groups made ongoing commitments to Nepalese charitable projects.

I had not lost my ambivalent view of the effect that exposure to Western ways has on Himalayan villagers. Although we may bring superior health care, electricity, and clean water, we also bring exposure to consumerism. There is an existential difference between villagers living in organic communities and Western postmoderns living in a consumer culture. Jacques Lacan and other postmodern philosophers make the point that anomie and alienation are increased by consumerism; I am what I consume, and nothing more. But many of us postmoderns find traditional cultures interesting and compelling. People living in traditional communities are defined more by relationships and what they produce and create, rather than by what they consume. This strikes a deep chord in those of us who feel the loss of the emotional honesty and interpersonal warmth of an organic community.

There is an attraction between Western and traditional cultures and peoples. Indigenous people desire what we have and we desire what makes them who they are. We have what will improve their lives in a material sense. But they have something we want: their sense of place, groundedness, and wholeness. Unfortunately, this relationship, even with the best of intentions, has too often resulted in destruction and distortion of indigenous culture.

It is perfectly understandable that Ang Temba wanted the benefit of piped water to his family's house. But what was lost to the community by families no longer gathering at the nearest river to fill their water buckets? We know in the States that increasing affluence leads to greater isolation behind the walls of gated communities. The more you have, the more you wall yourself off from your neighbors to protect what you have. When folks gather at a river to fill buckets or go to a local market to purchase food, friendly relations are created and maintained. Once the acquisitive process starts, however, the attractive power of increasing one's material wealth and comfort overwhelms community values and local customs.

When people in an indigenous culture embrace a tourist economy in the hope of obtaining greater material wealth, the danger is that they then become so like us, they lose their attraction and the tourists stop coming. The native people are then left with a damaged and distorted culture, and they don't even have the tourist dollar as compensation.

To find a middle way was my goal. By organizing worthy philanthropic projects for Himalayan villages and introducing curious and sensitive friends from the West to the culture of Nepal, I hoped to develop a healthy exchange between cultures. But would it be possible to have a wholly positive effect on the local people our groups encountered, or was it inevitable that we would be agents of further infection spreading the cancer of consumerism?

In general, I am plagued by ambivalence and find it hard to make commitments. I prefer to keep my options open. Yet I have come to understand that the most meaningful relationships in life are created through commitment, marriage and parenting being the most meaningful. Commitment requires faith despite feelings of doubt and ambivalence. So I decided to make a commitment to the plan despite my continuing doubts about whether it would help to promote a healthy relationship between Western friends and Nepalese or just lead to further exploitation and the spread of consumerism.

My faith in the commitment would be tested in a most amazing way in the 2008 expedition.

But back to 2003 and the Khumbu Sherpas . . .

3

RAPE OF THE MOTHER GODDESS

Sherpas call Mount Everest "Chomolungma," Mother Goddess. They know through their folklore that their ancestors came from the other side of Chomolungma, from Tibet, to settle in northeastern Nepal. Ethnologists have confirmed the truth of the Sherpa legend that more than 500 years ago they migrated from Tibet into what is now Nepal's Solu-Khumbu District. (The northern half of the district bordering Tibet is the Khumbu; the southern region is Solu.)

Mount Everest

While they lived below the mighty flanks of the highest mountain in the world, they did not attempt to climb or conquer her. They worshipped the goddess that lived within her. But the relationship with Chomolungma changed in the 20th century, when the King of Nepal began to let Western mountaineers into the Khumbu to try to climb the sacred mountain. Rather than resisting the assaults on her, the Sherpas welcomed the economic opportunities brought to them by the Mother Goddess.

Before Western explorers, adventurers, and climbers were allowed into the Khumbu, the Sherpas' economy was based primarily on yak herding and potato farming. So long as nature was not too harsh, the Sherpa way of life continued as it had for centuries, in tune with the changes that dictated where the yaks needed to be herded and when the potatoes needed to be planted and harvested. When the Westerners came, Sherpas at first served merely as porters for the exploration and mountaineering expeditions. The expeditionary style of mountaineering employed in the mid-20th century required an army of porters in a siege-like assault on the mountain. With their extraordinary strength for carrying heavy loads at high altitudes, Sherpas were naturals for the job. Their Western employers soon recognized other skills of the Sherpas, and they became cooks and guides as well. And when the West became serious about "conquering" Everest, a particularly talented Sherpa climber, Tenzing Norgay, was invited to participate as a member of the climbing team.

On May 29, 1953, Tenzing Norgay and Edmund Hillary became the first human beings known to stand upon the highest point on Earth. Within a generation of that first summit, Sherpa climbers became the dominant members of Everest climbing expeditions and hold most of the records for summits of Mount Everest. Some expeditions to Everest assign one Sherpa climbing guide to each paying client. Everest expeditions charge clients about $65,000, so they can afford to pay their Sherpa guides extremely well by Nepalese standards. (Remember, the average income in Nepal is about $1 per day.)

Serendipitously, when Hari and I hiked into base camp on May 26, 2003, to hang out with friends in the Nepal Mountain Madness expedition company, Lakhpa Gelu Sherpa, a member of the Mountain Madness team, had just returned to the camp after breaking the record for the fastest ascent/descent from base camp to summit and back. Lakhpa Gelu took "the standard route," pioneered by Hillary and Norgay, and reached the summit in ten hours and fifty-six minutes and then rapidly returned to base camp. His total round-trip time was eighteen hours and twenty minutes. I don't know what to compare this with in terms of amazing physical feats. Assuming no delays for bad weather or acclimatization problems, it takes most climbers at least seven to fourteen days to summit and return to Base Camp. Lakhpa Gelu completed in eighteen hours one of the most difficult feats

Everest speed climber Lakhpa Sherpa and me

performed by any human being, and one that at that time had been performed by fewer than 1,700.

Lakhpa, thirty-five years old when he accomplished this astounding feat, had first summited Everest in 1993 at age twenty-five. He told me he didn't do anything special to train for his record attempt. "Just climb mountains." He carried only eight to ten (rather than the typical thirty-five) kilograms of supplies in his pack. These consisted of an oxygen cannister, a brass plaque to place on the summit, a Nepalese flag, food, water, and a camera. He stopped to rest about ten times for two to three minutes. He left base camp at 5:00 p.m. on May 25 and returned at 11:20 a.m. on May 26. I interviewed him less than two hours after his return, at about one o'clock. I asked him what the record meant to him and why it was important.

He said, "Record is important because set on Golden Jubilee. I wanted to set record for several years, and wanted to do it this year. It is important that Sherpa set record. Sherpa are strong. We carry so much weight."

When I pressed him about what the record meant to him personally, he simply repeated that it was important that a Sherpa hold the record, and he wanted to do it for Sherpas and Nepal. When asked how he felt, he said his "upper legs and throat hurt a little."

Sherpa Ascendancy

Sherpa ascendancy to the top of the mountaineering world was paralleled by their economic ascendancy from one of the poorest ethnic groups in Nepal to one of the wealthiest. Sherpas were considered so insignificant among Nepal's fifty-some ethnic groups that they were just referred to as "the people of the east." There status changed as increasing numbers of trekkers and climbers came to the Khumbu after the historic first summit in May 1953. An average of 35,000 tourists per year entered Sagarmatha Park during the spring and fall trekking seasons in the 1990s. Consequently, comparatively large amounts of money entered the Khumbu in that decade. Within forty years of the first summit, the basis of the Sherpa economy along the Base Camp Trail had been transformed from yak herding to tourism. The hillbillies of Nepal became the nouveau riche.

The Mother Goddess brought the West to the Sherpas. From Western climbers, the Sherpas learned how to climb mountains. The Mother Goddess brought tourism to the Khumbu, and the Sherpas learned how to become tourist entrepreneurs. Some became quite wealthy, owning chains of lodges, airlines that fly trekkers and climbers from Katmandu into the Khumbu, and even an Internet café at Everest Base Camp. And the Mother Goddess? She has been desecrated with rubbish, oxygen canisters, and the dead bodies of failed climbers.

The ratio of deaths to successful summits of Everest is about one to ten. Next to the medical clinic in Pheriche, which is a few hiking stages south of base camp on the trail, there is a monument to climbers who have died attempting Everest. The last time I paid my respects at the monument in 2006, it had 250 names. About 2,500 climbers had successfully summited Everest by then.

One might be tempted to think the Sherpas great hypocrites, if all that was known of them was that they had exploited their goddess for profit. A friend, who is a schoolmaster in Sikkim and has worked to preserve traditional Buddhist practices and culture in Sikkim, calls the Sherpas of the Khumbu "whores." But Westerners who encounter Sherpas come away from the Khumbu extolling the virtues of these amazing people, whose character combines superhuman toughness with gentle Tibetan Buddhism. "They are the strongest, toughest, yet kind, friendly, and most gentle people I've ever met" is typical of the effusions about Sherpas by first-time trekkers. And such effusions come from old Himalayan hands as well. "It has been my privilege to work with and get to know these kind, generous, extraordinarily gifted people," Jim Whittaker, the first American to summit Mount Everest, gushed in a letter to *Outside* magazine (July 2003, p. 23.).

I understand my friend from Sikkim calling the Sherpas whores and hypocrites for exploiting a sacred goddess for material gain. But it would be even more hypocritical for a tourist-adventurer from the United States to criticize Sherpas for becoming intelligent opportunists seeking to improve their standard of living. Isn't that a fundamental human drive? Still in all, I can't help but mourn the increasing loss of the traditional Sherpa way of life as the Khumbu Sherpas become more like me.

Sherap Jangbu is the owner of the Panorama Lodge in Namche Bazaar, the commercial center of the Khumbu. I interviewed him for my article about the Jubilee Celebration in 2003. He wore neatly pressed Levis and a light blue cotton shirt with collar. He had a son in college in the United States. I particularly liked this quote from Sherap:

> Changes are always good and bad. Tourism gives better jobs and money. Fifty years ago we could only be porters and guides to the expeditions. Now we have doctors, pilots and we can go to Katmandu. But we don't have politicians. Not much interest in national politics in the Khumbu. We have our own way.

Sherap, like every Sherpa I interviewed, expressed deep gratitude to Hillary and the Himalayan Trust for the schools and medical clinics built in the Khumbu. But Sherap insisted that tourism was the major source of successful development in the Khumbu. Even the foundation's funding, he reasoned, was based on the success of tourism. "The people that gave the money were people who became interested in helping the Sherpa people after they visited the Khumbu. People liked the Sherpas and wanted to help us."

When I asked him whether there was any downside to the fifty years of changes, he sounded a note of ambivalence.

Men only wear traditional clothes for ceremonies. Modern clothes are easier to wear and warmer. Young people like modern ways. They're not as interested in singing and dancing. Kids in Katmandu don't even speak Sherpa. About one-half don't come back. But only four to five doctors are needed in the Khumbu, so we don't need all the doctors and engineers to come back. And now with the drop in tourism, there are too many lodges.

Every Sherpa I interviewed for the article agreed that the changes tourism brought to the Khumbu were well worth any cost to their culture. They uniformly insisted that the essential Sherpa character had not changed. When pushed, however, a note of nostalgia about "lost ways" would register. But the more pressing concern to Sherpas now dependent on tourism was, as Sherap Jangbu put it, "the drop in tourism." These Sherpas were divorced from the cycle of nature and now dependent on the cycle of the market, on Western money being brought into the Khumbu.

The worn and gentle face of Namche's most honored resident, Gyalzen Sherpa, was on the cover of the April 2003 issue of *Outside* magazine. Gyalzen was one of the high-altitude porters from the 1953 expedition. Only three of these porters were still alive in 2003.

As Hari and I walked the dusty streets of Namche to Gyalzen's house, Sherpani (female Sherpa) shop owners called our attention to their wares and a few young Sherpas played a game of dice on a street corner. We passed the Club Paradise, the highest pool bar in the world. The village was completely electrified and all the lodges, shops, and restaurants had running water. In 1998, I had seen the first light bulb in Namche turned on at the post office. In five years, Namche had been transformed. Tibetan traders still squatted on their haunches in the open-air market displaying yak-hair carpets they had carried around the Everest Massif, but Sherpanis now sold batteries and plastic climbing boots from shops with stone walls, electricity, and running water.

I brought the *Outside* magazine with the cover picture of Gyalzen to his house. Hari and I spent a convivial two hours with the eighty-five-year-old Gyalzen; his wife, Pemba Lagi Sherpa; his sister, Fur Diki Sherpa; and his youngest daughter, Ang Diki Sherpa. Our hosts treated us with typically warm Sherpa hospitality. Pemba Lagi kept our teacups full of salty yak-butter tea and kept insisting that we take another cookie from the tray she pushed toward us. Ang Diki sat on the floor beside my chair smiling up at me and nodding along with the conversation. Fur Diki sat in a corner, watching us contemplatively while fingering her prayer beads. Gyalzen was the center of attention and held court as the "monjo," the "big man" and unofficial mayor of Namche.

Gyalzen told us that he loved working as a high-altitude porter for the 1953 expedition. He is the eldest of the expedition's surviving high-altitude porters. He went up to the South Col with Hillary, and described that as "the best thing" he's done. "Staying in base camp was very nice." He said he was very happy Hillary had come back to Nepal for the fiftieth anniversary, and laughingly showed us the personal invitation he received from Hillary to come to the Jubilee Dinner in Katmandu cohosted by the king and Sir Edmund Hillary. He spoke of all that Hillary had done for the Sherpas. "We were very poor. Couldn't even speak Nepalese. There was nothing in Namche before Hillary. He brought schools, a hospital, and drinking water to Namche."

I asked what Tenzing had done for the Sherpas, and he responded that Tenzing "helped the world to know Sherpa culture. We were only known as 'people from the east.' Norgay made us Sherpa and known to the world."

Gyalzen related how the people from Namche followed "the white people" all the way to base camp just because the locals were so curious about these people with white hair (blonds) and who drank water from bottles. "They thought these people were very special and had special things. Some people followed the 'tourists' just to look at them."

He assured me that "no bad things have come from the 1953 summit" and the tourism that followed. "So many good things for Sherpas. Now there is a doctor and a pilot in Namche. The Sherpa people are still very strong. Still very friendly."

He was correct about the benefits of tourism for the Sherpas and that most Sherpas are still very strong and friendly, but there are now obese Sherpas who sit in shops and collect money; Sherpas who no longer look at white people with great curiosity but merely as a means for more revenue; and Sherpas who have grown up not learning the traditional songs, dances, and language.

The insidious power of consumerism has a leveling effect on all cultures. It demands uniformity. The same products are sold from Bangor to Bangalore. Nike, McDonald's, Hanes, and Starbucks goods are the same in Indianapolis and Katmandu. The assembly lines of multinational companies do not have the sensitivity or take the time to appreciate diversity among nations and cultures. Multinational media conglomerates spread the same "desirable" images around the globe. Beyonce is as big in Beijing as in Boston. Sherpas chose to transform their economy from a yak-based to a money-based economy, understandably. Despite the denials of most of my Sherpa acquaintances that their essential Sherpa character has not changed, I have found it difficult to agree with them.

Hiking to Khumjung the next day, we passed by the Everest View Hotel at Shyangboche. The hotel was built with its own helipad (the only private helipad in the Khumbu) in the early 1990s by Japanese entrepreneurs. The plan was that rich Japanese tourists would chopper up to a modern hotel with a view of Mount Everest without having to hike from Lukla. The story goes that all the guests in the first few groups to stay at the hotel became violently ill with altitude sickness because they flew from Katmandu at 5,000 feet to 12,500 feet without any time to acclimatize. The owners went bankrupt and all the locals lost their jobs. The restaurant at the hotel reopened a couple of years later, but the grand

View from the Everest View Hotel

but empty hotel stands as a symbol of the unfulfilled promise of never-ending economic development for the Khumbu Sherpas.

I took the accompanying photo at the Everest View Hotel restaurant in 2006 on what I thought would be my last trek in the Khumbu. The majesty of the highest peaks on Earth is forever memorialized in my memory, as are the gifts I have received from the Sherpa people of the Khumbu. My commitment required me to move on, to find a people and place in Nepal to which I could give back and from whom I could receive what the Sherpas living in a tourist economy can no longer give. I wanted to find a people and place in Nepal still living in harmony with the cycle of nature rather than living according to the market cycle and dependent on the tourist dollar.

4

WALKING TO SCHOOL

Niru Rai went to school one day. He had to walk two hours on steep mountainous trails from his home village of Basa in the Solu region to the nearest schoolhouse in the larger village of Sombare. What he learned from his single day of school was that he would rather get paid for walking long distances than walk to school. He left his village to find work as a porter with an expedition company and never returned to school. He worked his way up from porter to kitchen boy to cook to sirdar to company owner. But Niru did not lose touch with his home village. He married a village girl, built a home in the village, and began hiring men from his village to staff his growing expedition company. He didn't forget his lack of education and that the children growing up in his village still had to walk two hours to the nearest school.

The success of his company led to connections with Westerners and, in 2003, he convinced a French-Canadian NGO to supervise construction of a one-room schoolhouse in Basa village on land Niru donated. The Canadians were the first "white people" to enter the village of Basa.

I became acquainted with Niru Rai in 2006, the second year of my commitment to organize groups of friends for Nepal expeditions. In the fall of 2004, the commitment was fulfilled with a three-person trek in Langtang and climb of Yala peak. The expedition company we used was run by my friend Kafle, who also manages the NGO for which I raised $1,000 from friends and to which I delivered sixty-five pounds of donated school supplies and clothes in 2004. But in 2006, KP was on a fundraising trip in the United States for his NGO when I was trying to organize the next expedition. Unable to locate him, I looked for other Nepalese-owned companies that ran Gokyo-Lobuche expeditions. I discovered Niru's company, Adventure GeoTreks.

Niru provided ten references of Western clients, who raved about the quality of service he provided. The program Niru proposed fit well with my plan to trek through Gokyo, climb Lobuche East, and trek back to Lukla through Tengboche and Namche Bazaar. The proposed price was quite reasonable, so I contracted with him to run the 2006 expedition.

When we met in Katmandu in October 2006, I found a kindred soul in Niru. He cared deeply about giving Westerners a transformative experience in Nepal. And he hoped that some of his clients would be moved to do more for the people of Nepal than just spend money on a trek. Although I had studied and learned much about the Sherpa people, I knew almost nothing about Niru's people, the Rai.

In 2006 and 2007, despite the U.S. State Department's travel warnings about the danger of the Maoist revolution in Nepal, I organized expeditions through Niru's company with Ganesh Rai as our sirdar. Ganesh and most of the crew who staffed our expeditions were also from Basa village. The sense of community of these men and their exceptional care and concern for our group members fueled my growing interest in their ethnic group, the Rai, and their home village, Basa.

Ganesh and I became especially close on the 2006 expedition when the two of us climbed Pokalde Peak together. We had a permit to climb Lobuche East, but the other members of our group decided they didn't want to attempt the climb. Two were satisfied with just trekking and two were too tired near the end of the trek to attempt what would be their first Himalayan climb. So Ganesh and I took a day away from the group to "bandit climb" Pokalde. We didn't have a permit, but there were no other teams on the mountain the day we climbed.

Ganesh's strength, fortitude, and good humor amazed and delighted me. We slogged up 3,000 feet from base camp to a shoulder below the summit. We postholed through knee-deep snow and scrambled over rocky and loose scree without using crampons or ice axes, just humping and scrambling. From the shoulder to the summit is a fifty-foot rock climb at 19,000 feet. It was a thrill to follow Ganesh up that last bit, feeling for hand- and footholds above the clouds, with the Mother Goddess looking down on us from the other side of the valley. Standing on the summit, just the

Ganesh on Pokalde Peak

two of us, with no other human beings in sight, only other great whitecaps as far as we could see in all directions, was a special bonding moment.

On the hike from Pokalde Base Camp to the village of Dingboche, after our descent, we lost the trail. We were trying to take a shortcut when a blinding sleet storm blew over the moraine we were crossing. We lost the trail in blowing sleet. Having trekked for two weeks, climbed Pokalde, and then taken a rugged off-trail shortcut to Dingboche, my legs were shot. But Ganesh kept my spirits up by joking and laughing, and refused to let me descend into self-pitying whinging. As we reached the outskirts of Dingboche, he ran ahead as I stumped along, barely able to put one foot in front of the other. A shower tent with a hot bucket of water and ladle was waiting for me in camp, set up by Ganesh as I was clumping through Dingboche.

Ganesh, like other Nepalese sirdars I have known, embodies *in extremis* that wonderful combination of strength and compassion I have found in Himalayan mountain people. He also speaks Nepali, English, German, French, Italian, Spanish, Japanese, and more than ten dialects of local languages. This mastery of languages is typical of Nepalese sirdars. Those I have known have other admirable talents. My first sirdar, Ang Nima Sherpa, was a skilled thangka painter. Hari Pudasaini, my guide and interpreter for the Jubilee and our sirdar for the Langtang-Yala Peak expedition in 2004, could make a living as a stand-up comedian on the club circuit in the United States. Himalayan mountain guides grow up in mountain villages, learn the expedition business, and rise up through the ranks to the highest position within an expedition's crew. They must command the respect and loyalty of their crew as well as deal successfully with all varieties of modern Westerners. As a group, Nepalese sirdars are the finest examples of human beings I have encountered.

Over the Ganja La

In 2007, the greatest challenge of the expedition was getting our group members, our staff, and all our supplies and gear over the 17,000-foot Ganja La. Niru had warned that this pass would be difficult; very high and snow-covered, it requires ropes to cross. It was even more challenging than expected. We had hiked for two days in rain below the pass, which meant two days of snow building on top of the pass. The hike up to the top of the pass from the south was long and slow in deep snow, but not terribly steep. The real challenge was getting down the other side, as the descent was a sheer drop-off and the snow was even deeper on the north side of the pass.

It took several hours for Ganesh to figure out how to fix enough rope to get each member and all the staff and our supplies down the pass in thigh-deep snow. The temperature was drop-

Ganesh setting rope on Ganja La

ping and frostbite was becoming a concern as the trekkers and staff huddled on the crest of the pass. At least, hunkered down below the ridgeline, we were sheltered from the wind. Ganesh struggled alone and exposed out on a precipice, fixing rope. It appeared impossible and impassable, but despite the subfreezing temperature, deep snow, and blowing wind, Ganesh was able to fix ropes so we could rappel down the pass, glissading (sliding on our butts) the last fifty yards.

Several of our group members, and even a few of the younger crew members, described it as the coldest and hardest day of their lives. Despite working much harder than anyone else, Ganesh smiled, laughed, and encouraged the staff and group members to keep moving and to be careful. And he made sure that Ram, our cook, was able to brew tea and boil soup for everyone as soon as camp was set up. The physical and spiritual toughness of our group, following Ganesh's example, allowed all four members (three of whom were novice climbers) who attempted Yala Peak to stand on the 19,000-foot summit just two days after enduring the Ganja La.

When we returned to Katmandu after completing the expeditions in both 2006 and 2007, Niru and his family hosted our entire group at their home in Katmandu for a seven-course feast. Many toasts were offered, especially to Ganesh for being such an outstanding guide and spiritual leader, and to Niru for being such a splendid host and putting together all the pieces that gave both groups wonderful experiences in the Himalayas. It was striking to observe how Niru, this uneducated man from the remote mountain village of Basa, was able to conceptualize and execute a business plan so well that every client left Nepal feeling like their expectations had been met or exceeded. I also marveled at how easily Ganesh transmogrified from wilderness guide in the mountains to cultivated tour operator in Katmandu.

The Rai People

My curiosity about the Rai people and Basa village was increased. I wondered what the village was like that produced Niru, Ganesh, and a crew of men who demonstrated, to an extraordinarily high degree, the virtues of hard work and consideration for others.

I had learned from Ganesh, talking with him as we hiked miles and miles of trail together on two expeditions, that there are eleven different subgroups among the Rai people, each with its own local dialect. The deep valleys and high mountains of the Solu area, where most of the Rai live, created separate pockets of people, whose isolation from each other led to the development of different local languages. Most Rai follow a religion that Ganesh described as a "middle way," borrowing from animism, Hinduism, and Buddhism. He told me, however, that the Rai around Basa believe in an ultimate Supreme Being, unlike the other religions of the Indo-Tibetan Himalayas. They are animistic; that is, they believe that all things, animate or inanimate, have spirits. There is a giant kapok tree outside of Basa village that is sacred to the villagers and has become a place of worship. (When I saw James Cameron's *Avatar* I was blown away by the resemblance of Rai culture to that of the fictional Na'vi.)

The Rai have learned and tell the myths and stories of Hindu gods and legends, and to a limited extent, follow the caste system. But their values, customs, and mores are more similar to those of Tibetan Buddhism than Hinduism. Ethnologists claim the Rai migrated from Burma to Solu-Khumbu in ancient times, although their physiognomy looks Mongol (which to my eyes, interestingly, resembles the Mayan people of the Yucatan).

The British military recruits Rai into the famed Gurkha Battalion. To become a Gurkha is considered a great honor in Nepal as only the very toughest men from the high country are invited to join. Rai were among the Nepalese hill tribes that defeated the

Brits in 1812, when they first attempted to invade Nepal. British military leaders were so impressed with the skill and toughness of the hill tribes they offered Nepalese fighters from the middle Himalayan area, specifically from what is now the Solu region, the opportunity to enlist in the British military service. In 1815, 5,000 Nepalese hill dwellers, including many Rai, joined King George's "Gurkha Rifles." The Gurkhas are still an elite unit within the British military, specializing in mountain warfare and guerrilla tactics.

The Rai are as tough as the Sherpas, but since they live at lower altitudes and not along the Base Camp Trail, they were not recruited by the early Western expeditions for mountaineering. In order to benefit from the burgeoning trekking-tourist industry in Nepal, Rai people had to leave their villages to go to work for Western-owned and Sherpa-run companies. The popular trekking trails do not pass through areas populated by Rai. So in the 1970s and '80s, men like Niru, who wanted to work as porters for expedition companies, left their villages in Solu and hired on as "coolies" to work up north in the Khumbu or down south on the Annapurna Circuit. Their own villages remained largely untouched by Western tourism.

My attraction and admiration for the Rai of Basa village was similar to my feelings for the Sherpas when I first went to Nepal in 1995. They are the toughest and gentlest people I know.

Niru and Ganesh told me about the need of the Basa village school for physical plant improvements, educational materials, and basic supplies, and, most important, the hiring of two additional teachers so fourth and fifth grade classes could be added to the school program. When Niru asked whether I would consider organizing a trek to visit Basa in conjunction with developing a fundraising project for the school, I immediately agreed.

5

SHATTERED PEACE,
POVERTY, AND POLITICS

◦ॐ◦

Nepal is one of the poorest countries in the world. It runs neck and neck with Bangladesh in a race for the poorest country outside of Africa. The average annual income is about one dollar per day. Nepal does not have a public schools system, and the national literacy rate is below 50 percent. Although it has more than fifty distinguishable ethnic groups, each with its own language or dialect, most of the local-regional languages are preliterate. (Niru told me the Rai had a written language "in ancient times," but it was lost.) Despite its poverty and cultural diversity, tolerance and harmony among its different ethnic groups and castes has generally been the way of Nepal.

Nepal became an object of fascination in pop culture in the 1960s and '70s. A lax attitude toward hash and pot smoking combined with the custom of hospitality and tolerance by the Nepalese Hindu-Buddhist culture encouraged hippies and spiritual seekers to come to Katmandu. "Freak Street" near Thamel (the old town and tourist center of Katmandu) became an international destination for head shops. Local gurus and holy men were happy to take on paying students and devotees from the West. (My two favorite gurus, were the Milk Baba, who consumed no food or drink other than milk during his adult life, and the Penis Sadhu,

Sadhus at Pashupatinath

whose discipline was to lift with his penis a fifty-pound concrete block tied to a silk kata. The Penis Sadhu died a couple years ago, but the Milk Baba may still be visited at Pashupatinath.)

Love and peace, like the Beatles preached in "All You Need Is Love" and "Magical Mystery Tour," seemed to hip and enlightened Westerners to be embodied in Katmandu. Bob Seeger's 1975 hit "Katmandu" ("Goin' to Katmandu, that's what I'm gonna do") nailed the sentiment that Katmandu was where it was at.

The pop-culture view of Nepal was not entirely frivolous. Spirituality is a fundamental cultural value in Nepal. Gurus gather followers and may become cultural heroes as their popularity and renown grow. This is in contrast to the United States, where cultural heroes who gather devoted followers are more likely to be AM radio ranters than authentic spiritual leaders. The Rush Limbaughs of our culture gain popularity with divisive and mean-spirited rhetoric. A guru gains renown in Buddhist-Hindu culture through promoting the message of peace and love and encouraging followers to greater spiritual enlightenment.

In the 1960s and into the 1990s, Nepal was a beacon of peace in the sense that Hindus, Buddhists, Moslems, Christians, and all the different ethnic groups lived in peace. Religious coexistence, rather than religion-inspired violence, has been the guidepost of Nepal's history. Political strife and caste oppression are part of the country's history as well. There were coups and countercoups for and against the monarchy during the 19th and 20th centuries. But peaceful coexistence among its diverse ethnic population had been the norm since facing down the British invaders in the 19th century. The Maoist revolt against the kingdom, however, transformed Nepal from a peaceful Shangri-la to another place of terror and violence on the world stage.

A Change to Violence

In the 1980s and '90s, the trekking-tourist industry grew rapidly. Many Nepalese were lifted out of poverty in the tourist destination areas such as the Katmandu Valley, the Khumbu along the Base Camp Trail, Langtang, Pokhara, and around the Annapurna Circuit Trail. But the boom was short-lived and busted by the end of the '90s. The 2003 Jubilee celebrations caused an uptick, but the truce between the government and the Maoist rebels ended after the celebrations, and the return to violence again scared off the tourists, particularly Americans, because President Bush declared the Maoists an international terrorist organization.

In October 2004, while I was mucking around in Tribhuvan International Airport dealing with lost bags, friend Elliot was waiting for me outside the airport when he saw an explosion in downtown Katmandu. The Maoists had rolled three hand grenades into an office building. That was the closest anyone in my trekking groups came to experiencing violence or being directly affected by the civil war in Nepal. But fear of violence and the political instability of Nepal frightened some friends away from joining expeditions.

Beginning in the late 1990s, the Maoists claimed territorial rights over certain trekking trails. These trekking trails became revenue sources for the Maoists. Armed bands would block trails and require trekkers to pay a fee to use the trail. The leader of the band would give the trekkers a lecture about politics in Nepal and then issue each trekker a certificate declaring the fee had been paid so other Maoist bands would not collect the fee a second time. If a trekker didn't have enough money to pay the fee, the Maoists would take a camera, climbing gear, down jackets, or other valuable possessions. The fee was generally around $100, but after the U.S. government declared the Maoists international terrorists, Americans were required to pay double the amount of all other nationals. When the Maoist insurgency was at its worst, I wrote "Canada" on my trekking duffel with a Sharpie, just in case.

The Maoists were unsuccessful in penetrating Sherpa communities in the Khumbu, so, happily, I never had an encounter with one of their armed bands. Every Westerner I met in Nepal who hiked the Annapurna Circuit from the mid-90s through 2006 had a Maoist encounter. In the Khumbu, what we encountered was an ever-increasing military presence. Each year, we passed more government soldiers on the trails and had to cross through additional military checkpoints.

In Katmandu, the king would periodically impose a curfew on citizens, which usually didn't apply to tourists. Walking back to our hotel in 2004 after a night out with Nepalese friends, Briggie, Elliot, and I had to endure the hard stares of young soldiers with loaded carbines. They were understandably resentful that we were allowed to walk the streets of Katmandu freely, while our

Nepalese friends had to skulk down alleys and hide from the soldiers, or risk arrest or a beating. Most of the army recruits during the civil war were young uneducated village boys. Their training was poor, evidenced by the fact that they lost most of the pitched battles against the Maoists, and the allegiance of the Nepalese people eroded and eventually swung in favor of the Maoists. So it sent a little shiver down my spine when that young soldier stepped out in front of us, pointing his rifle at us, while intently eyeballing Briggie, a tall, slim, blond, blue-eyed South African. But with a sneer and jerk of his head, he let us pass.

In 2004, the first year I organized a trekking group, five people who had planned to join the group chickened out due to State Department warnings. In 2006, two women canceled two days before departure because of riots against the king breaking out in Katmandu. Of course, we are all prisoner to our own experience regarding fear of crime and violence. South Africans Elliot and Briggie were highly amused at American fears of violence in Nepal. Even with the civil war raging, they found Nepal much safer than Johannesburg, which has one of the highest street crime rates in the world.

I have never been the victim or even seen any real violence in Nepal, but what I did experience was amazement and disbelief at the change in the Nepalese attitude toward violence as the Maoist rebellion became a full-fledged civil war. Just before my first visit to Nepal in 1995, a Nepalese guy killed a European in a bar fight in Katmandu. The entire nation was in mourning when we arrived because of the felt national disgrace and sorrow over a guest of Nepal being killed. In the ten-year civil war, from 1996 to 2006, an estimated 12,800 Nepalis died. I found it unbelievable that the Maoists and the government could have brought such a degree of fear, death, and destruction to a nation that mourned so soulfully over the death of one person two years before the war began.

In 2006, as the war reached its climax, a friend was brutally beaten in Katmandu. Raaj is a native Nepali, but grew up in India, has long hair, owned a tea shop in Katmandu, and is the leader of a rock band. He looks like a dissident, but he was not a Maoist, just a guy who loves Western rock music. One night when walking home after a gig in Thamel, Raaj and his band mates were jumped and beaten by "royalists." Raaj's arm and nose were broken. When I saw him a month or so after the beating, of course I was upset for him, but I also found it hard to accept that such a thing could happen in this country that had been a beacon of peace in a violent world just a few years before.

Maoists and the King

The assessment of most of my educated Nepalese friends is that, although the Maoists started the war and brought death and terror to Nepal, it was the arrogance, incompetence, and brutality of King Gyanendra that inspired so many to join the revolt to bring down the government. Gyanendra, King Birendra's younger brother, became king after Crown Prince Dipendra shot and killed his parents and siblings at the dinner table on June 1, 2001, after arguing with his parents about a girlfriend. Dipendra turned the gun on himself and was in a coma for three days before dying. As King Birendra's eldest son, Dipendra was legally king for the three days he spent in a coma.

King Birendra had been a fairly popular king. Although the Maoist revolt began several years before Dipendra's patricide, it was largely contained in the rural west. After Gyanendra was crowned, he vowed to crush the rebels with the overwhelming military superiority of the army. Instead, the army repeatedly lost battles to the guerrillas and the rebellion spread across the country as Gyanendra's heavy-handed rule turned more and more Nepalese against the king.

The Maoists were not popular among my educated Nepalese friends in Katmandu. One friend compared the Maoists to the Mafia with a political agenda. He told me his experience was typical. The Maoists had a cadre member in my friend's village, a suburb of Katmandu, and the local Maoist representative required every villager to contribute money or food to the Maoist cause. Any family that refused to contribute to the Maoists risked having their house burned down, being beaten, or even killed. To an American like me, who had lived in Chicago, it sounded just like a protection racket.

Another friend, who managed a hotel in Katmandu, told me the hotel paid extortion money to the Maoists in order not to be hassled or to have a hand grenade tossed into the lobby. A third friend, whose son was studying medicine in the United States, had to hide that fact from her neighbors for fear the local Maoist cadre would think she could pay extortion. She feared the Maoists would reason that, if she could afford to send a child to study in America, she could afford to contribute to the cause. Her son was on a full scholarship, but she doubted the Maoists would care about that.

No, the Maoists were not seen as saviors by the educated classes or those benefiting from the developing tourist economy. They were very popular, however, among the poor in western Nepal, which had no tourist industry and was neglected by the government. Over time, the Maoists' popularity increased across different sectors of the country's underclasses. The elite and high castes dominated the parliamentary parties. With the Maoists, the poor of Nepal finally had a party that claimed to represent them, and the Maoists were the only party demanding that the despised King Gyanendra be deposed.

By 2006, the country was so weary of the war, furious with King Gyanendra, and frustrated that the Parliament had been unable to establish a road map to peace that thousands took to the streets in Katmandu. Gyanendra tried at first to suppress the demonstrations with force, but the demonstrators refused to back down and thousands more joined the demonstrations against him. The day before my group arrived in October 2006, the king agreed to give up executive power, the Maoists agreed to participate in elections, and the Parliament agreed that a new constitution would be written. By May 28, 2008, Gyanendra was deposed and the 500-year-old Shahi dynasty came to an end. The new constitution created a parliamentary democracy, and the Maoists won a plurality of the vote in the first election. The chairman of the Communist Party of Nepal (the Maoist's formal party name), a man known as Prachanda, was elected prime minister and thus became the first democratically elected Maoist leader of any country.

World leaders wrestling with problems of insurgencies and civil unrest could learn from Nepal. It took ten years, but the issues tearing the country apart have been largely resolved. Nepal rid itself of an oppressive executive power, the king, and incorporated the insurgents, the Maoists, into the government after they agreed to disarm and participate in UN-supervised elections. The former insurgents became the dominant party in the Parliament, but since they did not win an outright majority, they have to cooperate and negotiate with other parties. After less than a year in office, Prachanda resigned as prime minister in a dispute with other parties over control of the military. But he did so without bloodshed because the revolutionaries were enmeshed in the political process. The lesson is that entrenched ruling elites who do not serve the greater good must be driven out and the revolutionaries then brought into a democratic process.

◌ ▦ ◉ ◌ ▣

When our group arrived in 2006, just after the king had backed down to the Katmandu demonstrators, the country was in a celebratory mood. The demonstrators and military had left the streets and the vendors, local shoppers, and tourists had returned. When we arrived in 2008, there was a growing confidence that peace had returned to Nepal. The despised king was gone, the Maoists had successfully participated in elections judged fair by neutral observers, and the Maoist fighters had laid down their arms under UN supervision.

Far from the Modern World

So much history had occurred in just a few years. None of it, Niru and Ganesh told me, had any effect on Basa village. According to them, Basa had been virtually unchanged for 500 years. No electricity or running water and nothing moved on wheels around Basa. It's only experience of all the history that had roared through Katmandu in the previous decade was stories brought home by the men who worked for Niru's expedition company.

Niru and Ganesh told me that if I was able to organize a group to come to Basa, we would be only the third group of "white people" to visit Basa. The second group was French and they had supervised the building of a small addition to the school building in the spring of 2008. The first was the French-Canadian group that worked with the villagers to build the school in 2003. The idea of a trek off the tourist trails to a village with no electricity, running water, machinery, or wheels and nearly untouched by the modern world intrigued and excited me.

Most of the Sherpa villages in the Khumbu had developed electricity and water systems by 2003. I interviewed Ang Rita Sherpa, who runs a lodge in Pheriche along the Base Camp Trail, when I stayed with him on my way to Everest Base Camp during the Jubilee celebrations. He was worried about the downturn in tourism caused by the civil war and exacerbated by 9/11. I asked what he would do if his business failed. He said his family would have to return to herding yaks and growing potatoes and barley.

"Before tourism, Sherpa people very poor," he said. "Traded with Tibetans and took crops to Namche to trade. Now we can buy things with money. I don't know if business will get better. Just wait and see. If we have to return to farming, we have land here. This is Sherpa home. Can't go anywhere else."

But I didn't really believe that he would just return to the life of his ancestors. The power of a money-based and consumer-oriented economy is too seductive. I doubted he could simply let go of it. More likely, he would fight and scrabble to find a way to hang on to the gains in creature comfort that tourism had brought to his family.

I understood Ang Rita's fear and his desire for a more comfortable life. Wouldn't I feel the same in his situation? Hadn't I spent much of my adult life striving to acquire more money and a higher level of comfort for my family?

That is exactly why I wanted to experience Basa and see a village living a way of life similar to what the Sherpas had lost. And I could give back to the village of my friends and help children for generations by improving the village school. Niru had calculated that if $5,000 could be raised for the school, all needed improvements could be made and fourth and fifth grade teachers could be hired for the school. My spirit of adventure and curiosity might be slaked by a trek to Basa and my commitment to help Nepalese villagers could be fulfilled by a fundraising project for the school. So instead of planning a climbing expedition as I had originally intended, before I left Nepal in 2007, Niru and I began to develop a plan for an October 2008 trekking expedition to Basa village and a fundraiser for the school.

6

ORGANIZING FOR BASA

While Ganesh attended to organizing the crew and retrieving the ropes we used to rappel down the Ganja La, Ram, our cook, and I hiked out ahead of the group to try to find a good campsite for the night. It was a relief to be over the 17,000-foot pass, but the sun was going down and we had to hike over a moraine in thigh-deep snow. It was hard and tricky, postholing through deep snow and occasionally breaking through a hidden snow-covered hole or small crevasse and cracking a knee on rock. Every level spot I found, Ram nixed as an acceptable campsite for one reason or another. After an eternity, well, at least an hour or two, of frustrating searching in growing darkness for a site satisfactory to the finicky Ram, Deepak, one of the assistant sirdars, caught up with us. Ganesh had settled on one of the sites Ram had rejected. Hiking back, I broke through the snow once more and again cracked my right shin on a rock.

While the crew assembled tents and set up camp, the members of our group hugged each other for warmth, huddled on a plastic tarp Ganesh had ordered spread out as an extra barrier between our butts and the snow. Ram and his kitchen staff brewed tea and boiled soup. No one got frostbite, but Jim and Cindy, two very experienced backpackers and leaders of the Central Indiana Wilderness Club, described waiting for the soup

Glissading down the mountainside beyond the Ganja La

and tea after descending the Ganja La as "the absolute coldest" they'd ever been. My hiking boots and gaiters were frozen solid. They were still so stiff the next morning, even after smashing the boots together several times, they felt like they had turned into concrete. Shoving my feet into those blocks of ice was not the most pleasant way to start the day.

The next day, we hiked into the village of Kyanjin after rappelling and glissading down another high snow-covered pass. I was too damn weary to join the four of our nine-member group who hiked off the following morning to climb 19,000-foot Yala Peak. I was conflicted about passing on the climb, because I was supposed to be the group leader and Yala is a beautiful beginner peak with a two- or three-hour glacier slog, twenty-foot rock climb just below the summit, and final knife-edge ridge crossing to reach the summit. But Elliot had climbed Yala with Briggie and me in 2004, and both Ganesh and our Sherpa climbing guide, Lakhpa, would be there for the group, so I decided I would just be a drag on the team.

Five of us explored the 900-year-old Kyanjin Gompa (monastery), and then Tim Meyer, Jim Farless, and I hiked up a river and over Kyanjin glacier above the village. After Jim hiked back to the village, I told Tim about the idea Ganesh, Niru, and I had been tossing around for developing a fundraising campaign for the Basa village school and planning a trek to Basa.

The 2007 expedition was Tim's first experience of Nepal, Asia, or the Himalayas. He is also a leader in the Central Indiana Wilderness Club and an experienced outdoorsman. Nepal struck a chord in him. Other obligations would prevent him from joining the trek to Basa in 2008, but when I told him about the fundraising, he offered to be the first contributor. He was as worn out as I was after Ganja La, and one might have thought he would have been put off by the hardship of the trek and could care less about the village school of the men who herded us over the torturous Ganja La. (Tim had confided after about the fifth day on the trek that it was the "hardest thing" he'd ever done.) But Nepal, the Himalayas, and Niru's crew have an opening-up, rather than a closing-in, effect on people. Tim was happy to offer to help with the fundraising campaign, and he was indeed the first to contribute after we returned to the States.

Tim and I hiked around the glacier and then back to the village, where we visited shops of local weavers and traders. While we were wandering around, we met three local Tamang women who asked us to choose two of them to marry, so we could have a "Coke wedding." (Tamang is the dominant ethnic group in the Langtang area, and they claim to be descendents of Genghis Khan's horsemen.) This request was a new one on me, and Tim and I were both curious to find out what a Coke wedding was. Through sign language and my rudimentary Nepali, and with much giggling among the women, we discerned that they wanted us to buy them Coca Colas. They thought we would be more willing to buy Cokes for them if they were willing to marry us. We declined the marriage proposals, but Tim did buy the three of them Cokes.

The School Project

After our return from Nepal at the end of October in 2007, I began the task of organizing the fundraising campaign for the school project along with organizing a trek to Basa. At first, I spent a great deal of time trying to find a tax-exempt organization that would oversee the project, so I could just act as the fundraiser. Using a tax-exempt organization as the "funnel" for funding the project would allow donors to claim a charitable deduction. Unfortunately, I discovered that there are numerous organizations interested in being the beneficiary of a fundraising effort, but I could not find one that would facilitate all the money raised going to the school project. For example, Engineers Without Borders was interested in helping but wanted to spend a portion of the funds raised to pay to fly a supervisor over to Nepal and to provide room and board for the supervisor. Those costs would have eaten up about half of the $5,000 I hoped to raise. A few other organizations were interested in helping but wanted 10 to 25 percent of the funds raised as an administrative charge or to divert a percentage of the funds to some purpose other than for the school.

It made no sense to me to pay to send a supervisor to Nepal or to allocate a significant amount of the funds for purposes other than improving the Basa school. Niru would supervise the work on the ground in Nepal and I would raise the funds, so how would it help the children of Basa to spend money on an unnecessary supervisor or to pay money to an organization that was only needed to provide a charitable deduction for donors? It was frustrating because I knew the people involved with the organizations I contacted cared deeply about helping Himalayan villagers; that's why they were involved in these nonprofit organizations. But each organization had its own agenda, and Basa was not on the list.

I considered dropping the project. I had enough on my own plate organizing and recruiting for the trek, not to mention running a law office, doing my share of raising two teenage boys, trying to be a responsible husband, and everything else that an active modern American does. Hell, I still had my doubts about whether I would really be doing Basa village a favor by helping to educate their kids. But I had made a commitment to Niru and to this village I had not even seen, so I put my head down and slogged forward, just like trudging up one of those never-ending Himalayan glaciers. I gave up looking for help from an established organization. I would just do it myself.

Niru told me that the French NGO, Sol Himal, had enlarged the school building in the spring of 2008. The original building was a three-room schoolhouse for first through third grades. Now there were rooms for fourth and fifth grade classes but no funds to pay two more teachers. Niru informed me that it was government policy to take over the payment of village teacher salaries if the village established a school and found a way to pay the teachers for three years. Niru had paid the salaries of the teachers for grades one through three for the mandatory three years, but he didn't want to take on the obligation of two additional teachers.

He also reported that the original school building needed repairs, including replacement of door and window frames, patching a badly cracked cement floor, building a safety wall beside the building where there was a steep drop-off, and clearing ground in front of the school for a playground. Niru was confident that $5,000 would provide sufficient funding to pay for all that was needed, including the salaries for the two additional teachers. The plan was for the villagers, under Niru's supervision, to do the repair and construction work themselves. Two women from the village had been trained as teachers and were ready to begin teaching fourth and fifth grades.

Before I asked friends to donate money to the project, I wanted to make sure there would be safeguards for oversight of the funds after the money was transferred to Katmandu. I had become friends with the president of the Katmandu Lions Club, Uttam Phuyall. Uttam is the senior manager of the Katmandu Guest House, where I have stayed each time I have been in Katmandu since my 2003 Jubilee trek. Uttam is also the local agent for two Western nonprofit organizations and is one of the most considerate and thoughtful people I know. I asked Uttam if he would be willing to be cotrustee with Niru on an account for the project. Uttam and Niru had become acquainted through Niru's booking of my group members at the Katmandu Guest House. After I described the project and what Niru had already given to the school, Uttam was happy to help. In late January 2008, I began emailing and calling friends, asking them to make a $25 to $500 donation to the Basa School Project.

I also began recruiting members for an October 2008 trek. The expedition Niru and I planned would be an eleven-day cultural trek. We would fly to a village airstrip at Phaplu in the Solu region west of Basa, and then do a circuit trek, stopping at various villages, gompas (monasteries), and cultural sites along the way back to Phaplu, and then fly back to Katmandu, where we would conclude the expedition with a day tour of the Katmandu Valley. The program would be an introductory trek that would not be extremely challenging, so we could attract folks who might not be hardened outdoorsmen like my Wilderness Club friends on the 2007 expedition but who would enjoy a cultural trek and might be interested in joining the effort to raise money for the

Basa School Project. The highlight of the cultural trek would be two days and nights in Basa halfway through the trek.

Both campaigns, to recruit donors for the school project and members for the trek, went well during the winter. But unforeseen obstacles to both efforts arose as summer came and departure for Nepal in October neared.

My initial pitch to prospective donors was that I was only asking for a pledge of $25 to $500 at this point. I would go to Basa in October, inspect the school, interview the teachers, and set up the bank account with Niru and Uttam. After my return, I would ask for the pledges to be paid to an escrow account, assuming the donors were satisfied with the report I brought back from Nepal. After the $5,000 was raised, I would wire the funds to the trust account Uttam and Niru would open with a bank in Katmandu.

By summer, I had raised $4,000 ($1,400 in actual donations from friends who didn't care to await my report from Nepal and the rest in pledges). But the fundraising had stalled and I had no leads on additional donors for the shortfall of $1,000, until I saw a guy walking toward the fitness room at my YMCA branch, wearing climbing boots and gaiters.

Serendipity

Normally, I would have been outside biking, rollerblading, kayaking, swimming, or running for my workout on a summer day, but rain and luck, fate, or karma had driven me inside to work out and to meet Bob Meyer. Bob appeared to be about fifty and extremely fit; I later learned he was actually almost sixty. I asked him what mountain climb he was training for. He was impressed that I recognized the purpose of calf-high plastic boots and gaiters. He told me most people stared curiously at his climbing boots and asked why he was working out in ski boots. Bob told me he was training to climb Cho Oyu, a 26,750-foot peak west of Mount Everest in Tibet. His climb was planned for the fall.

It is a rare sight to see someone in the flatlands of Indiana training for a big mountain climb. For several years, I was 50 percent of the Hoosier membership of the American Alpine Club, the preeminent association for American climbers. The other member was my friend Tom Proctor, who led and organized the climbs I did in 1998 and '99 (1999 was the ill-fated Mera Peak expedition).

Bob and I continued our conversation as we pounded away on Stairmasters in the Y fitness room. I told him about the trek I was planning to lead and the fundraising project. I detected more than just a spark of interest in Bob's eyes. I learned that he had been to Nepal once before and that his team would be back in Katmandu, after the Cho Oyu expedition ended, the same week my group was to arrive in Katmandu.

We saw each other a few more times over the course of the summer working out at the Y or on the Monon Trail, a greenways trail that runs about twenty miles through Indianapolis. We continued our conversation about Nepal and my interest in helping Basa village. Bob told me he would like to help with the fundraising project but wouldn't be able to focus on any other commitments until his return to Indy after his attempt on Cho Oyu. But he said he'd have the administrator of his charitable foundation contact me to talk about a possible donation.

Bob was a man of means with a commitment to philanthropy and a heart for the people who live in the high regions of the Himalayas. Through our conversations and email correspondence during the summer of 2008, it became clear to me that he understood the dilemma and my concern over trying to help without harming the culture of Himalayan villagers. We agreed that one of the best ways to help was through the education of kids, who would then have the freedom to choose whether to remain in their traditional culture, leave it, or bring something more to it that they gained through education. We also agreed we would try to meet in Katmandu, so he could tell me about the climb on Cho Oyu.

As summer ran its course and tree leaves began changing from uniform green to the extravagant colors of fall in Indiana, I had no further success in finding more donors for the school project. It seemed as though my solo efforts at raising $5,000 would fail. Maybe my own doubts were undermining my efforts. Maybe prospective donors were feeling the impending collapse of our economy in 2008 and wanted to hang on to their money. Whatever the reasons, I hated the idea of telling Niru I had been unsuccessful, but that seemed to be the case.

Late in the summer, the administrator for Bob Meyer's foundation called and told me Bob wanted to donate $1,000, which would bring the fundraising to its goal. The foundation trust rules required, however, that funds could only be disbursed to tax-exempt organizations. A few weeks before, I would have torn my hair in frustration on account of the many fruitless overtures I'd made to nonprofits. But fortune had smiled on the project, as another friend through my YMCA had offered to allow his family's 501(c)(3) organization to act as the sponsor for the project.

I had served on the board of managers for the Jordan branch of the YMCA for several years. That summer Brad Bloom served on the branch's Christian Emphasis Committee, which I chaired. I knew his family ran a not-for-profit school in Bloomington, Indiana. When I told him about the village school in Nepal for which I was raising funds, his eyes did not glaze over. He was interested. And when I told him the story of my failed efforts to find an organization through which to funnel the funds, he was happy to help because one of the purposes of his family's organization was to educate needy children. It was a serendipitous break.

So all donations to the Basa School Project would be made to Brad's family corporation, La Campagne Ministries, which would then transfer the funds to the trust account in Katmandu. This arrangement would allow all donors to take a charitable deduction for their contributions. La Campagne would only charge a 1 percent administrative fee plus any banking fees incurred, so the arrangement would almost be a pass-through for the school. A mutually beneficial sidelight of the arrangement for Brad and me was that La Campagne Ministries is the parent affiliate of Lifestyle Media Group, which publishes *Faith & Fitness Magazine* and *Map: A Travel Lifestyle Magazine*. I agreed to write gratis for the magazines a couple of articles about trekking in Nepal. We hoped the articles would generate prospects for the trek to Basa as well as additional donations to the School Project.

Best of all, since the arrangement with Brad's corporation satisfied the administrator of Bob's foundation, a pledge of $1,000 was received and, woohoo, we surpassed our goal of $5,000!

Chapter 7

GOIN' TO KATMANDU

᪥

Organizing the trekking group had its problems and surprises too. Ten members originally signed up for the trek to Basa. Niru and I were both very pleased with this increase from our 2007 nine-member Langtang-Helambu trek.

It was a good group. Two high school teachers from the Indianapolis area planned to do a comparative study of education in Nepal. John, a physician friend from the Jordan YMCA, would be a useful addition to the group, as a medical doctor is always a valuable member of any expedition. Dr. John planned to bring a load of medical supplies to donate to the medical clinic nearest to Basa, which Niru had advised is in Sombare, a two-hour hike from Basa. I had not seen my cousin David, who lives in the LA area, since he was a little kid, but he had heard of my Himalayan experiences through the family grapevine, and he reconnected with me to ask if he could join my next expedition. Two friends of friends, Karen and George from Biloxi, signed up. Bill, a friend from college now living in San Diego; Carl, a member of the Wilderness Club; and Dax, a veteran of many climbing and trekking expeditions and my tent mate on my first climbing expedition in Ladakh, India, completed the group.

But by the time we arrived in Katmandu, the group was only six. The two teachers had been counting on a grant for partial funding of their costs, but it was denied, so they had to cancel. Dr. John was in a car wreck just a month before our departure date. He cracked several ribs and was in no condition to trek and sleep in a tent. George from Biloxi had planned to lose weight but didn't, and so decided he was not sufficiently conditioned to handle the trek.

Each year, I tell the group members that to handle a standard Himalayan trek they need to be able to do at least forty-five minutes at a good, hard pace at a steep uphill setting on a Stairmaster or elliptical machine, and, to handle an introductory climb, they need to be able to do at least sixty minutes. George knew he wasn't in shape to handle the trek, and he was wise enough to bow out.

The six of us arrived in Katmandu on different dates and by varying routes and airlines. Karen flew the Atlantic route on India Air with a stop in Delhi. Dax came through Dubai on the Emirates airline. Bill and I flew from Los Angeles on Cathay Pacific. Carl was the first to arrive in Katmandu and had flown Royal Thai Airlines. He had planned to spend several days in Katmandu before the trek started to acclimatize and explore Katmandu. David was the last to arrive on October 6, 2008, the day before we were to fly up into the mountains.

Katmandu is a cultural shock to first-timers with its wild tuk-tuk drivers, rickshaws, women in colorful saris, lepers, and beggars. Given the 5,000-foot altitude, it is helpful to arrive in Katmandu at least a couple of days before starting the trek, especially for those who live at sea level, to acclimatize and to become acquainted with the local culture. It also allows time to do gear sorting and to shop locally for any needed gear, clothes, or personal effects for the trek.

Only one other member of the group, Dax, had been to Nepal and had mountaineering or trekking experience. I met Dax in 1996 at the Hotel Imperial in New Delhi. He was just under six feet tall and weighed over 225 pounds, massively muscled in the upper body. Dax was a weight lifter who wanted to become a mountain climber. On our first Himalayan climb, we were hotel roommates as well as tent mates. Just after we met in the hotel lobby, Dax told me he had talked management into an upgrade for our room, and then he said, "You do know what I am?" I had guessed. Dax became my New York Jewish weight lifter, mountain climber, gay friend.

Bill and I met in college. He was the best friend of another friend of mine. We all went to law school after we graduated from college but began our law practices in different places, Bill in San Diego. We got together a few times in a group of mutual friends from college. The group took ski trips to Big Bear in California and fishing trips in the Sea of Cortez. After Bill moved to California, he developed an interest in Hispanic culture, becoming fluent in Spanish and marrying a Mexican woman. Bill was someone who was sensitive to and enjoyed cultural differences, I thought.

I met Carl through the Central Indiana Wilderness Club but had not done any Wilderness Club trips with him and did not really know him. He is six foot six, so a giant by Nepalese standards, an actuary, and a very spiritual guy. Karen was a friend of one of my neighbors. I didn't meet her until we arrived in Katmandu but had learned through email correspondence that she was a psychotherapist, was very interested in spiritual matters, and used the nickname of Narayani, which is the name of a powerful mother goddess in the Hindu pantheon.

The group members had not known each other before joining the trip, though some were able to meet before leaving the States for Katmandu. We met for the first time as a group at dinner at Thamel House Restaurant the night before we were supposed to fly into the mountains. Niru made a quick appearance to meet the group, but he was hosting a larger group at another restaurant. Niru's son, Milan, and Sanga, who would be our sirdar, hosted the dinner. Sanga led the Katmandu day tours our groups had done in 2006 and '07, but I had not done a trek with him. I was disappointed that Ganesh was guiding a climb on Dhaulagiri, a 26,810-foot peak in western Nepal, and could not be our sirdar. But Sanga's English is slightly better than Ganesh's, and he has the kind and comforting temperament of Nepalese sirdars that I admire, so I was confident he would do the job well. Like Ganesh, he is married to a sister of Niru. I learned subsequently that Sanga's wife is the head teacher at the Basa school.

We met Niru for breakfast the next morning at the Katmandu Guest House (KGH), and I presented him with a check for the $1,400 already in hand for the school project. As is often the case, a couple of our members needed to rent sleeping bags, so we walked to a gear rental shop in Thamel owned by a friend of Niru. Climbing gear and trekking supplies can be rented or purchased at secondhand shops in Thamel for a fraction of the price it costs to buy the same items in the States, so I encourage those who don't own some needed gear to buy or rent after arriving in Katmandu. (The one item each member absolutely must have before arrival is a well-broken-in pair of hiking boots.) A trip to a gear shop has become a first-day ritual for my groups. Exploring the narrow streets of Thamel together provides another opportunity for the members of the group to become better acquainted.

After a leisurely day of walking and shopping, we met Sanga back at the KGH, where he distributed the company-provided duffels we would each use on the trek and answered last-minute questions about packing the duffels. The porters will find a way to carry anything and any amount of weight a member of the group wants to bring on the trek, but there is a forty-five-pound weight limit on most domestic flights in Nepal. That should not be a problem for trekkers, but climbers have more gear and often must wear their climbing boots and multiple layers of clothes on the flight up to the mountains. Irrationally, the forty-five-pound limit is based only on baggage weight. What a passenger wears or carries is not considered in the weight limit.

Niru had sent our group members a detailed list of recommended items to bring on the trek along with a list of items and amenities provided by his company. His list is accurate down to the number of socks, underwear, and reading materials, so I encourage members to use the list as their bible for packing. Nevertheless, some members seem unable to follow these simple directions. In 2006, one member brought a Coleman stove, cooking pots, plates, and utensils, even though Niru's list clearly stated that all food preparation is done by the staff and members need bring nothing in the way of food or utensils other than snacks or power bars. One of our porters carried this group member's "kitchen" on the sixteen-day trek, even though it was never used.

Katmandu Culture

The next morning, we met Sanga in the KGH lobby, expecting to be driven to the airport to fly to Phaplu, the village airstrip that was to be the starting point of our cultural trek. Bad news: although the sky was overcast only in the Katmandu Valley, lightning was flashing up in the mountains and most of the flights that day, including ours, were canceled. Since we had planned to do a day tour after our return, Sanga suggested we use this day instead. That way, we would remain on schedule for the departure dates from Katmandu. We agreed, piled into the van, and drove off to see the strange and quirky sights of Katmandu.

We visited Swayambodh, "the Monkey Temple," where arrogant monkeys stalk around a magnificently eclectic Hindu-Buddhist temple complex overlooking the city. We walked the sacred circuit around Bodnath, the largest Buddhist stupa in Nepal. Sanga and I showed the group how to turn the prayer wheels clockwise, according to Buddhist tradition, and to chant the Tibetan-Buddhist prayer for good luck, "*Om mani padme hum.*" While we ate lunch atop a restaurant overlooking the gigantic stupa, men climbed to its peak and threw buckets of whitewash and gold paint over the sparkling white structure. We spent most of the afternoon hiking around, sitting for a while across the Baghmati River from Pashupatinath, where the ashes of all devout Hindus in the Katmandu Valley are carried to the sacred Ganges.

In a Hindu funeral, priests prepare and then burn the bodies one after another on ghats, cremation platforms, on the bank of the river below the temple complex. So many corpses are burned each day on the ghats that it looks like a ceremonial assembly line. The ashes of the cremated body are stirred by the priest's

Pashupatinath Cremation

Bringing Progress to Paradise

great stick and then scuffed into the river. Trash and the bodies of dogs and monkeys float down the river, while pilgrims and sadhus bathe just upriver from the ghats. The scene offends Western sensibilities of hygiene. But lest we become too stiff-necked about our superior ways, Sanga pointed out that above the ghats is the oldest known hospice in the world. While Hindus have been coming to Pashupatinath for a thousand years to prepare for death by spending their final days with family and spiritual advisors, it has only been in the last few decades that the West has discovered the wisdom of this approach to death.

A surprising development during our group's tour of Katmandu was that my old friend Bill frequently complained about the carelessness and stupidity of Nepalese drivers. When he was bumped on the arm by a rickshaw in Thamel, he yelled at the driver, as if he thought the rickshaw driver had done it deliberately. Then he complained about the incessant honking and about tuk-tuks weaving in and out of lanes. He was upset that Nepalese drivers were not behaving according to his American standards of traffic etiquette. Fortunately, the other trekkers enjoyed the tour.

That evening we met Bob Meyer for dinner at a restaurant in Thamel that Bob suggested. The restaurant was fairly busy and the service was slow, but I was enjoying Bob's description of his successful but scary climb of Cho Oyu. Drinking chiyaa (tea) and chang (beer) while we awaited our food, the group was having convivial conversation getting to know each other and Bob, I thought. Bill, however, was becoming increasingly upset about the food not being served. After about foty-five minutes, he stood up and declared he was leaving and asked Karen to leave with him. She politely declined. I tried to mollify Bill, pointing out that the evening was pleasant, we were seated outside, and there was no need to be in a hurry. Bill stayed but remained agitated, and only calmed down after Bob paid for the entire group's dinner.

Bill was manifesting symptoms of "the ugly American." It made no sense to me. He is married to a Latina, his kids are bilingual, and the family lives cross-culturally, with homes in both San Diego and Mexico. And he is one of the nicest guys I know. Yet he seemed more concerned about unregulated traffic and slow service than the cultural experiences offered in a country new to him. It seemed as though he expected Nepalese to conform to his standards, rather than being curious to learn about their ways. He even mocked local customs and language. The common greeting in Nepal is "namaste," which is usually translated as "I recognize the god in you." It is a lovely greeting and sentiment. Most words in Nepali are stressed or accented on the first syllable, as is namaste. At every opportunity, Bill used the greeting but exaggeratedly stressed the last syllable instead of the first, mispronouncing it "nam-us-stay!" Then he would chuckle, laughing at his little joke. He was a different person in Katmandu from the friend I had known.

Tim Meyer told me that on his flight from LA to Katmandu for our 2007 expedition, he sat beside a Nepalese businessman. Tim asked the fellow what advice he could offer to one who had not been to Nepal before. The Nepalese guy said, "Open your mind." That was excellent advice and I passed it on to our group in 2008. But the message wasn't reaching Bill.

It also worried me that Bill appeared to be about thirty pounds overweight and walked with a slight limp. He had assured me several weeks before we left for Katmandu that he had been working out, hiking up and down hills around his home. When Dax and I had visited him in February, eight months before the trek, we both stressed that he needed to lose weight and get in shape if he was serious about joining us on a Himalayan trek.

When he called me in May and said he'd decided to join the group, he asked me to promise him that Dax and I would look out for him and "not leave him up in the mountains." I assured him he would not be left behind, but it would not be Dax or me that would be responsible for his safety, it would be our sirdar and crew. And I told him the best insurance of doing well on the trek was to get in the best shape he could by working on his cardio-aerobic conditioning and leg strength. "You need to have the heart and lungs and leg strength to get up mountain trails higher than you have ever been in your life." It was the same message I gave each member of the group. But the importance of the advice had not penetrated Bill's consciousness. His lack of concern for the demands of the trek seemed to reflect his lack of respect for the local culture.

A Change of Plans

In the morning, we assembled again with our duffels in the KGH lobby, ready for the drive to the airport. Sanga wasn't there yet, so we focused our attention on the TV in the lobby. A news station was reporting that the first morning flight to Lukla had crashed. When Sanga arrived, he gathered us around him and told us that all the morning flights into the mountains were canceled due to the plane crash. We were to meet again in the lobby after lunch to find out whether we could get a flight out that day.

As we waited, we monitored the news about the crash in Lukla. It was not good.

Flying into Lukla at 7,000 feet is an adventure in itself. As the prop plane approaches the runway, you see a sheer mountain face below it and a sheer mountain face at the runway's end. If the pilot comes in too low, the plane will crash into the mountain below and, if too high, it will crash into the rock face at the end of the landing strip. When a plane flies out of Lukla, the plane actually drops off the end of the airstrip, because of the sheer mountain face at the end of the short runway, and then the plane gains altitude. Before the airstrip was resurfaced and widened in 2006, there was a fence between the airstrip and a farmer's field made of broken props, wings, and tails from downed planes. I morbidly enjoy the reaction of first-timers when I point out the fence after landing in Lukla. I don't enjoy, however, recalling a terrible night in Lukla in 1998, awaiting news about our lodge manager's son, who was in a helicopter that crashed on the flight up to Lukla. Early in the morning, the news arrived that there were no survivors.

On the other hand, while the experience of flying in and out of Lukla is harrowing and exciting, if you look out the windows of the plane on a clear day after it gains altitude, you can see the highest mountains in the world in their great and majestic beauty.

By the time Sanga returned after lunch, the news reports were that the pilot had come in too low and crashed into the mountain face below the airstrip. No survivors were expected. There would be no more flights that day, and, because so many flights had been canceled in two days, Sanga feared we would be unable to get a flight for another two days. The group was sobered by the crash and there was actually relief among some members of the group when Sanga informed us we would be unable to meet our expedition deadlines if we awaited another flight.

Sanga told us he had put together two alternative itineraries and asked us to choose between them: an Annapurna trek or taking a bus as close as we could get to Basa and then hiking to Basa. The Annapurna trek would be a teahouse trek, meaning we would stay in lodges, because our tents, kitchen, cook, and porters were in Phaplu waiting to meet us. If we took a bus to Jiri and then began hiking to Basa, we would spend the first two nights in lodges, but would then meet our crew on the trail and tent camp to Basa and then back to Phaplu for our flight out.

The trek to Basa would not be a leisurely cultural trek, however. Sanga explained that the bus would leave us at least two days this side of Phaplu, where our flight had been scheduled to drop us. The trek had been planned as an introductory village trek. It would now become an extreme trek in terms of the distance we would have to hike each day. Sanga estimated that our average trekking day would increase from the planned four to six hours to six to ten hours and we would have no rest days. Alternatively, the Annapurna trek would be a more leisurely trek with similar hiking distances to what we had planned.

I very much wanted to go to Basa. The primary goal of the trek for me was to visit the village, inspect the school, and bring back a report to the prospective donors to the school project. Of course, I hoped our group would have a great experience and I thought that visiting a village as untouched by the West as Basa would be the climax of the experience for our group. So I told the group how I felt, but we would vote and the majority would decide. I wanted to be fair and truly let the group decide the issue. I explained to them that I had not been to Annapurna, but after the Khumbu Base Camp Trail, it was considered the most beautiful hike in Nepal.

There was little discussion. We had already lost two days and were all anxious to get on the trail. The vote was unanimous to go to Basa.

Though I had shared with the group my strong desire to see Basa and the school, I hadn't shared with them a murmuring disquiet in the back of my mind about how we might be the harbingers of a transformation of Basa by being the first actual tourists to visit Basa. The French-Canadian and French groups who had been to Basa before us had not come as tourists. They were secular missionaries there to work on the school building. True, I was raising money for the school, but our group was on a tourist trek, not a philanthropy mission. How would we affect Basa by being its first tourist visitors? By opening Basa to tourism, were Niru and I really doing the right thing for the village?

8

ON THE ROAD TO JIRI

As we gathered in the lobby of the Katmandu Guest House to await Sanga and the bus, Carl and Bill were still screwing around with their duffels. My immediate concern was to make sure everyone was prepared to leave the hotel when the bus arrived. We would be gone for eight days. I was energized by the anticipation of getting out of the polluted air of Katmandu and into the mountains.

After our unanimous vote to trek to Basa, Sanga and I had told the other members what they needed to do to be ready for the bus the morning of our delayed departure. Everyone needed their passports on the trek, but they should leave any unnecessary documents and valuables in the hotel safe. Sufficient currency should have been exchanged into Nepali rupees for the trek, hotel keys turned in, and each member's return registration confirmed with the hotel management. Duffels were supposed to be packed and extra luggage already checked into the KGH storage room. While I scurried around trying to make sure everyone would be ready for the bus and getting myself checked out of the hotel, I noticed Bill was still struggling with his duffel. I wasn't sure why Carl had his open beside Bill's. Bill looked nervous and Carl looked a little put out. But I had my own issues to attend to, so I just reminded them they needed to have their shit together by the time Sanga told us to load up.

Carl later told me that Bill had so much stuff in his duffel he couldn't close the zipper. Bill had three pillows in his duffel, including a pink one with built-in headphones. Niru's gear list stated that the company provided a pillow on the trek for anyone who needed one, so there was no need to bring a pillow, let alone three pillows. So, while the rest of us were checking out of the hotel, Carl was kindly making space in his duffel to accommodate some of Bill's excess baggage.

I realized I was becoming irritated with Bill, and perhaps beyond what was reasonable. When Sanga said the bus was ready for us, Bill wanted to stop everything and take a group picture in front of the KGH. I was getting antsy to get on the road, and we could have taken a group picture at the hotel anytime in the last two days, but of course, Sanga smiled agreeably and helped Bill get everyone arranged into a satisfactory pose. My irritation did seem excessive for the minor delay. Bill was thinking about preserving the moment, while I was concentrated on getting through it to begin the next moment—the road trip.

Anyway, we were off, but almost as soon as the bus moved into traffic in the narrow streets of Thamel, there was a minor accident in front of us. That sort of thing is just life in Katmandu. Minor accidents are common in my experience, but I have never seen a traffic accident with serious bodily injury in Katmandu. But now it was Bill who was upset; he began demanding that our driver get off this street. Sanga smiled and laughed as if he thought Bill must be joking, but he got out of the bus and helped the motorcyclist who had been bumped by a car move his motorcycle out of the way so we could pass.

Once we were out of the Katmandu Valley, the road trip became typical of driving in rural Nepal—a long, hazardous ride up and down narrow, winding roads through many one-rooster villages. Though the road to Jiri is dirt for stretches, it is mostly paved, constructed with funds provided by a Swiss organization.

Traffic drives on the left as in England and India, the two countries that have had the most influence on Nepal. Pedestrians in towns walk in front of vehicles with impunity, not, I think, out of ill intent, but out of a sense that moving quickly is not of particular importance. Roadway villages are usually a crappy-looking conglomeration of tin shanties thrown up around older stone and wood structures, with the occasional petrol station, tire repair shop, and roadside eatery with bhat (rice), chiyaa (tea), and chang (beer).

Roadside villages in the Himalayan foothills, as in most Third World countries, are a collection of poor people trying to eke out a living connected in some way with the commerce passing on the highway. Many have left nearby farms. The roadside villages above the Katmandu Valley are not aesthetically appealing to most eyes, but they are usually surrounded by lush green hills terraced with little farm plots of rice, millet, or barley. These pretty little farms mediate the contrast between the ugliness of human poverty inside the village and the beauty of nature's hills and valleys. When people mass into close quarters to try to live off of commerce, the result seems to be ugliness. It may be pastoral romanticism, but it also seems to me that when people live off the bounty of the land in small groupings, they enhance the beauty of the earth, rather than detracting from it.

I was really looking forward to getting out of the city, off the roads, and onto mountain trails, trekking through villages that cannot be reached by motor vehicles.

Group Dynamics

The group dynamics of expeditions can range from warm and comradely to interesting to volatile. As the bus ride from Katmandu to Jiri was twelve hours and we had already spent more than two days together, our group dynamics were taking shape. This group had only one woman, Karen, an attractive thirty-five-year-old brunette. From the first day in Katmandu, Bill paid particular attention to Karen, calling her "sweetheart," and making a point of sitting by her and walking with her. Sexual tension is always an interesting dynamic. I doubted anything would come of Bill's attentiveness to Karen, as he was a bald, overweight, over-fifty married man. I assumed he would not be particularly attractive to Karen. She, however, seemed to enjoy Bill's attention. Bill is clever, bright, and a gentleman. But I was worried that the growing fondness between Bill and Karen would add a dimension of difficulty to the hoped-for cohesiveness of our group. No one else seemed bothered, so I wrote it off as another symptom of my irrational irritation with Bill.

As we traveled east away from the Katmandu Valley and deeper into the Himalayan foothills, the scenery became more engaging. The road followed the Sun Kosi (River of Gold), which we eventually crossed by a steel suspension bridge. Then the road wound through and out of a great valley created by the river. Our driver carefully negotiated switchbacks up the side of the valley until we were tracking along the ridgeline road.

David showed us his impressive set of camera gear and lenses as we bumped along in our little bus. He does photography for the LA Galaxy soccer team, and was clearly the most practiced and prepared of all the shutter bugs in the group.

Scenic photo ops became more frequent. One town we drove through, Dolkha, had the Communist hammer and sickle symbol painted in red on many of its buildings. Sanga nodded and said, "Maoists," in response to our questioning looks.

Carl asked Sanga to tell us about the history of the Maoist rebellion. While Sanga described the bloody revolt that ended with King Gyanendra being deposed, there were different reactions among the group members. Carl listened attentively. Karen asked whether there was a spiritual dimension to the civil war. David listened with a cocked ear but continued looking out the window for scenic photo opportunities. Bill wanted to argue a few points about the socioeconomic causes of the revolt. Dax butted in a few times, trying to bring the history lesson to a close.

Dax was impatient to bring the attention of the group back to its primary focus during the long bus ride, which was Dax. During the ride, Dax engaged in almost nonstop comedic and intentionally inflammatory commentary. Dax loves to get under other people's skin. He is a loquacious New Yorker transplanted to LA and enjoyed outtalking the laconic Hoosiers, Carl, Bill (originally from Indiana), and me; the laidback Californian, David; and Karen with her languid Mississippi drawl. If he senses any homophobia, Dax makes sure to play up his gayness; if he senses an effort to show one's liberal acceptance of gays, he makes jokes about gays.

But more than just making jokes, Dax talks, and talks, and he doesn't stop talking. Once he gets going, it is like a dam has broken and words flood out in an unrelenting torrent. He mostly talks about himself—what he likes in food, his taste in clothing, the latest redecoration of his house, the real estate prices in his neighborhood, his most recent car or motorcycle purchase. Occasionally, he will interrupt the flow to ask your opinion, or to allow comment by another, but he will deftly cut off the interlocutor and (to mix a metaphor) gallop off in some other direction, paying no attention to what was said. Dax does this with complete self-consciousness and knowledge of the effect on others, and while he was holding forth on the bus, every now and then he would smile slyly at me or wink, to let me know, I think, not to take offense; he was just doing his Dax thing to properly introduce the rest of the group to what they had to look forward to on the trail with Dax.

Dax and I had been tent mates in Ladakh in 1996 and friends since then. We corresponded by email, visited each other a couple of times, and spent two days rock climbing the Gunks in upstate New York a few years after our '96 expedition. (The drive to the Gunks from New York City in Dax's new yellow Porsche Carrera was a trip!) And Dax was a member of our 2007 Langtang-Helambu expedition. He had been a good friend. And despite his exterior display of narcissism, when needed, Dax is a good listener and caretaker.

Dax was unable to do the climb of Kanglachen in '96. He was so heavy with upper body muscle that he was very slow and unsteady on the trail, got severely sunburned and dehydrated, and had mild altitude sickness before we reached base camp. Our leader, John Roskelley, ordered Dax, over Dax's strong objections, to hike out of the mountains with a group of Israelis who were on their way out and had four-wheel drive vehicles awaiting them for the drive back to Leh. Dax considered this experience humiliating, although he knew John's decision was the correct one. Over the next year, Dax shed forty pounds of muscle, trimmed down to 185, ramped up his cardio-aerobic training and left behind the bodybuilder lifestyle to become an outdoorsman.

If one is in the right mood, Dax is delightfully funny when he does his comedic-irritating schtick. If not, he's just irritating. Our group of six plus Sanga were happy to be on the road to Jiri in our little white Tata bus. And Sanga's happy-sirdar disposition set the tone, so for the most part, we enjoyed Dax on that twelve-hour bus ride.

The bemused but confused look on Sanga's face when Dax made gay jokes or references told me that he didn't really understand what was going on, but, like a good sirdar, he would laugh at whatever the rest of us laughed at. When we had a moment alone, Sanga asked me to explain Dax. Sanga had not had a gay member in any of his groups, at least that he knew of. He was shocked and intrigued when I explained that Dax is a homosexual. He treated Dax no differently after our private talk. In a tone of urgency to me, however, Sanga requested that we not let the villagers in Basa know that Dax is homosexual. He said, "They would not understand it."

We arrived in Jiri well after dark. Sanga directed our driver to a lodge on the main street. We pulled our duffels off the bus, and the lodge owner directed us to three rooms on the second floor. The rooms were the typical for Himalayan mountain lodges: plywood-walled cubes with a window.

Bill offered to share a room with Karen. When he discovered she had brought a battery-powered sound machine with her because she cannot sleep without its soothing oceanic music, he immediately asked Carl to trade rooms. Accommodating Carl placidly agreed, so Bill and Dax shared a room, as did David and I. In the morning and during the rest of the trek, many jibes were made at Karen's expense about her sound machine. "You come across the world to sleep outdoors in the Himalayas and bring a machine so you can hear the ocean, jeez!" She took the criticism in good humor and, each night on the trek, lapping ocean sounds were heard from her tent, perhaps for the first time in the Himalayas.

It was a good night for me, getting to know my cuz. We peed together standing atop the second floor ledge—male bonding.

The next morning, a little brouhaha broke out in Dax and Bill's room. Dax discovered that Bill had brought four pairs of blue jeans and a pillow collection. He was incensed that Bill expected a porter to carry these useless items on the trek. Blue jeans, like pillows, were not on Niru's list of items to bring on the trek. The most inappropriate pants one could pick for trekking are blue jeans; they are too heavy, too hot, and too tight to move comfortably on mountain trails. What was Bill thinking! Why did he ignore Niru's clear directions of what to bring on the trek? I never got an answer to that question from Bill.

Dax reamed him out, lecturing him on the fact that another human being would be carrying Bill's overstuffed duffel loaded with useless stuff. After dressing him down, Dax sorted through Bill's duffel, picked out appropriate clothing, and then ordered Bill to dress "like Jeff and I do on the trek." Fortunately, Bill had brought one pair of wind pants, which he wore every day after that.

But the sun was shining, we could see the mountains beyond Jiri, and we ate a large hot breakfast of bacon, eggs, and toast at the lodge. Off we went, our first day on the trail to Basa.

9

TREKKING WITHOUT PORTERS

I was very glad the group chose to trek to Basa rather than Annapurna. I wanted to visit the school, deliver the school supplies I had brought, and then report back to friends who had made donations or pledges to the school project. Selfishly, I also much prefer tent camping to staying in lodges. The Annapurna trek would have been a lodge trek. The route to Basa would, however, be much different from the one Niru and I had originally planned.

Sanga's new plan was to stay in a lodge in Jiri the first night and another lodge the second night in a village called Deorali. Then we would tent camp on the way to Basa and back to the airfield in Phaplu. Our route would be almost a straight line east from Jiri to Basa through Phaplu and then back to Phaplu, rather than the circular route Niru had planned, commencing with a flight to Phaplu. Much of our hiking on this impromptu route would not be on trails used by trekkers. We would be humping "locals only" trails to Basa. Niru had sent our porters to Phaplu with the tents and gear, expecting us to arrive there by plane. So we wouldn't have tents and a cook until we could meet up with our crew of porters, cook, and kitchen boys somewhere between Jiri and Phaplu.

Per Sanga's instructions, we left our duffels at the lodge in Jiri. He told us that Niru had called our cook, Purna Rai, by satellite phone just before we left Katmandu to drive to Jiri and told him to send our porters from Phaplu to Jiri. The porters were supposed to pick up our duffels at the lodge in Jiri and meet us in Deorali by the end of our first day of hiking. This would be an amazing feat by the porters, and how amazing it was would become clearer to our group over the next twenty-four hours. We were hiking with light daypacks, carrying only a change of clothes and personal kit. Our porters would hike from Phaplu to Jiri, which Sanga said would take almost two days, and then pick up our heavy duffels and hike the trail we were on now at a pace fast enough to catch up with us before we arrived in Deorali. Members of our group asked how it was possible for the porters to hike fast enough to catch up with us when they would each be carrying a heavy load and we were only carrying daypacks.

Sanga laughed at the question. The crew had left Phaplu as soon as we had decided that we were changing plans and taking the bus to Jiri. So they started hiking the afternoon before we left Katmandu. That meant they were about a half-day of hiking away from Jiri as we were leaving Jiri on our first day of hiking. After the porters arrived in Jiri, they would pick up the duffels and hike through the night if necessary. But still, we asked, how could the porters carrying our heavy duffels catch up to us tonight, while we only carried daypacks and they had not yet arrived in Jiri to pick up our duffels? Sanga laughed again; "The porters, they will take shortcuts."

Feats of Strength

I have seen amazing sights on Himalayan trails of porters carrying unbelievably heavy loads on mountain trails. I have seen porters carrying loads of lumber and rock that appeared to weigh as much as two hundred pounds. Most Nepalese porters are be-

Commercial transport in the Himalayas: porter carrying lumber

tween five foot two and five foot six in height and weigh 120 to 140 pounds. A recent study sponsored by *National Geographic* found that porters carrying loads into Namche Bazaar in the Khumbu carry weight on average equal to 93 percent of the porter's body weight. In 1998, I saw a porter literally running down the trail, carrying in his doko a six-foot-four German climber who had fallen sick at Everest Base Camp.

A doko is a straw basket the porters use to carry loads. It has a cloth strap or "tumpline" that fits over the porter's forehead and is long enough that the doko rides on the porter's back but is primarily supported by the weight being distributed down the porter's spine from the forehead. Some dokos have strings attached to the sides of the basket so the porter can shift the weight from side to side without stopping. Dokos do not have shoulder straps, like Western backpacks. Many porters carry a staff, called a "tokma," which is used for support and balance on steep up- or downhill trails.

Sometimes porters will stop for a brief rest by placing the tokma under the bottom of the doko to take the weight of the load off the porter's forehead. The resting porter will just stand there on the trail breathing hard for a couple of minutes, then pull the tokma out from under the doko and start walking up the trail. For longer rests, they will set down the doko and squat or lie down by the side of the trail. Porters are the tractor-trailers of the Himalayas, moving all the loads for expeditions and construction projects. Their only competition is the yak.

The *National Geographic* study reached no conclusion as to the source of strength that allows Nepalese porters to carry such heavy burdens. It is a mystery. Living at higher altitudes certainly helps but is not by itself a sufficient explanation. Some claim that nature or nurture has endowed high-altitude Himalayan dwellers with a higher red blood cell count than sea-level dwellers. I don't know, but I do know that Western trekkers who become acclimatized to high altitude cannot perform similar feats of strength and endurance. These small people are able to carry loads equal to their own body weight on steep rocky trails wearing cheap Chinese-made sneakers or flip-flops, or even barefoot. Only the most elite and well-trained Western climbers can handle comparable challenges, and they do it wearing high-tech boots and using the best backpacks and clothing that money can buy.

Porters typically wear handmade clothes or clothes given to them by members of expeditions they worked. If there is no lodge by an expedition campsite, porters will sleep in caves or huddled together in the corner of a rock wall. They might get to sleep in the meal or kitchen tent on some expeditions, but tents are not provided for porters on expeditions. Neither are sleepeing bags. If porters are allowed to sleep in a lodge, it is usually on the floor in the dining room, not in sleeping rooms. For food, porters carry cloth bags of rice tucked into their shirts or pants. They cook the rice in tins over an open fire and eat rice every meal. Porters are paid $4 to $8 per day.

Treatment of porters has improved over the last ten years as the government of Nepal has passed regulations requiring expedition companies to provide proper footwear, gloves, and sunglasses if the expedition is to trek above the snow line. Niru's company provided complete outfits of yellow and red wind pants and hooded windbreakers for our porters on the 2006 and 2007 expeditions. (That was another reason I was impressed with Adventure GeoTreks and have continued to work with Niru.) Several of the porters on the 2007 expedition lost or sold their gloves and/or sunglasses before we reached the high passes, but luckily Dax had several extra pairs of both and we were able to scavenge from our group enough gloves and sunglasses to outfit all of the porters before we reached the Ganja La.

Some trekkers feel guilty about the porters in their crew being treated, to some extent, like pack animals. But we get past it, and we certainly don't offer to take a turn carrying a porter's load. Considerate trekkers will do their best to keep the porters' burdens as light as possible by only bringing necessities on expeditions. Inconsiderate trekkers will bring things like extra pillows and useless Coleman stoves, which the porters will uncomplainingly carry every day of the trek.

I have been on two expeditions when there was a porters' "strike." On one, the porters refused to continue carrying until they received part of their pay, because they learned the company was having financial problems and they were afraid they would not be paid at the end of the trek. On Mera Peak, the porters accompanying us to high camp refused to go any farther up the mountain when blizzard conditions set in. They just put down their loads and refused to move. We were struggling along a knife-edge ridge after dark, and it was damn dangerous and scary.

The porters had better sense than our guide and leader. Tom, the leader, broke a tent pole over his knee in rage, but the porters had the final word and we set up camp where they demanded.

In 2003, when I trekked the Base Camp Trail with Hari for three weeks, I carried about forty-five pounds and Hari carried about fifty-five pounds. We didn't hire porters, until the last day for the hike out. Well, I hired one; Hari didn't. I ran, skipping and dancing down the trail on that last day it felt so good to be released from the burden of all that weight, which was only 25 to 30 percent of my body weight.

It is customary on the first rest day of a trek for novice trekkers to try to walk a little way with a porter's doko, just to see what it feels like to carry the porter's load. Most trekkers are unable to stand up unassisted with the loaded doko strapped to the forehead. But it is usually surprising to the trekker that the weight on the load distributed down the spine does not cause acute and excruciating neck or back pain. The system somehow works, but it is still unimaginable for a Western trekker to walk all day carrying a fully loaded doko.

The Eastern Way

My climbing partner in the 1990s, Tom Proctor, who was the leader of the 1999 Mera expedition, spent two six-month periods in Nepal while he was managing a guiding company. So he had more experience and a deeper insight into the minds of Nepalese porters than I did. We speculated about, and asked, what porters think about while they are walking all day carrying their loads. They don't have iPods with earbuds to listen to music. And they generally don't talk while carrying; they wait until they take a break to converse with their fellows. The senior porter who worked two expeditions with Tom and me in the '90s, Jid Baldoo, told us, "We think about our families. We think about how we will use the money we earn. We sing, and we chant *Om mani padme hum.*" His younger cousin, Man Baldoo, who was the rascal of our crew, butted in and said, "We think about wicky wicky [sex]!"

Porter at rest

One might think these answers show a commonality between the Nepalese and the Western mind. But there is a difference. What goes through the minds of American truck drivers on long hauls? Yes, family, how they will spend their earnings, and sex, for sure. But truckers have radios, CBs, CDs, cell phones, adjustable seats, heat and air conditioning, and rest stops with beds and showers. No doubt, truck drivers work hard. But there is such a difference between the outside stimulation a trucker and a Nepalese porter can access; and there is such a difference in the level of comfort a trucker has compared to a porter. The experience in the porter's mind must be much different. The porter has his own mind and the sound of nature to listen to. The trucker has many sources of stimulation other than his own mind, and he cannot hear nature over the roar of his engine and radio.

Porters on the Everest Base Camp Trail

I believe the essential difference between the Himalayan porter and American trucker is the former's calmness and acceptance of what the Western mind interprets as hardship. I have never seen a porter try to run another person off a trail or behave in a way equivalent to blasting an air horn or flipping the bird; I haven't seen trail rage. But I've seen, and experienced myself, plenty of road rage on U.S. highways and streets. The Tibetan-Buddhist traditions of the Himalayan mountain people develop a different character and mindset. Constant stimulation is not needed; a more meditative state is comfortable. Passivity or acceptance of one's lot in life, as opposed to striving for more comfort, is the common attitude.

While gurus and yogis preach the Eastern philosophy of acceptance and not striving in exchange for a nice retainer fee from affluent Western devotees, Himalayan porters live it. I am not promoting the Eastern way as necessarily superior to the Western way, and I'm certainly not recommending that American accountants and lawyers leave their practices to work as coolies in Asia. Without ambition and striving, the West would not have produced the Parthenon, the Sistine Chapel, the Moon walk (Armstrong's and Jackson's), and "My Girl" by the Temptations. But I do agree with the Dalai Lama and certain New Age teachers that we can learn from the Eastern way; and we are in some respects.

The East has learned from us as well. Leftist economists make much of the deleterious effects of globalism and multinationalism on developing countries. But Third World leaders and businessmen of good faith see their efforts at economic development as helpful to their communities and countries. Niru certainly does. These leaders are trying to integrate Western ways into their local economies. The trick is to take what is best from the West and blend it with what is best from the East. Economic development that improves the standard of living, provides better health care and education, is, in most minds, certainly my Sherpa friends', good. But in my view, it is only good if it can be achieved without loss of meaning and breakdown of community in the indigenous and traditional cultures affected by development. So far, there are not many successful examples.

The West may be having a more successful go of it in integrating some of the wisdom of the East. I wrote the "My Turn" article for *Newsweek* (November 25, 2002), "The Revolution You Won't See on TV," which makes the claim that the American legal system is undergoing a quiet revolution, moving from a conflict and competition-based system to a cooperative mediation-based system. A significant factor in this transformation is the demographic fact that women are taking over the legal system as more women than men now graduate from law schools. So it's not surprising that a cultural shift within the system has begun toward a more feminine-nurturing approach to problem solving. The feminization of the legal system has helped promote a more Eastern attitude of cooperation through mediation and a de-emphasis on the conflict-based method of trial by litigation.

This cultural shift in the West is affecting more than the legal system. The Dalai Lama is one of the most revered figures in the West, because his message of peace, cooperation, and peaceful resolution of disputes is resonant with the growing understanding of many in the West. The '60s pop culture message of peace and love promoted by hippies, who were influenced by Eastern philosophy, has not been extinguished. It has been moving subterraneanously through Western consciousness and surfacing in unlikely places such as the legal system and perhaps even the White House in the election of our first multicultural president.

It is no wonder we find Himalayan culture so attractive. Although the porters, who embody the Eastern way so concretely, are poor and even pathetic to Western eyes, they are also very special to us. They are stronger and yet gentler than we are. They amaze us.

10

FIRST DAY ON THE TRAIL: DEATH MARCH TO DEORALI

The sun was out and it was already warm on an almost cloudless day as we hiked out of Jiri. It had rained during the night and was a humid morning. The trail out of Jiri was wide and more like an unpaved Indiana country road than the Himalayan trails I had hiked on other expeditions. Sanga explained that a motorway was planned and the first stage of the trail had been leveled into an unpaved roadbed.

Children laughed and waved to us as we passed their plaster-walled and tin-roofed homes. A few local people hurried by. As the trail wound around and then rose above the town, it narrowed and became steeper and more difficult. The country was lush; mixed deciduous and pine forest and thick, green, bushy undergrowth surrounded the trail. This terrain of the Middle Himalayas looked to me more like the rain forests I've hiked in Belize, Honduras, and Puerto Rico than the stark and rocky High Himalayas where I have spent most of my time in Nepal.

Bill was struggling up the first long, steep incline we encountered just beyond the outskirts of Jiri. His face was red and he was sweating profusely. He alternated between wearing a bush hat and putting a wet washcloth on his bald pate. I was worried about him. If he struggled this hard the first morning on the first steep section of trail, how would he be able to handle the higher altitudes and the long days ahead?

David seemed to be doing fine. Karen was flushed and her stride wasn't much better than Bill's. Her gait was awkward, as though her hiking boots didn't fit well. They were unmarked and looked new. I wondered if she had properly broken in the boots. Carl was a little stronger, but somewhat unsteady on his long legs and size 17 hiking boots. Dax was reveling in his superior fitness, talking a mile a minute, and making sure the others noticed how easily he was trekking along. He rolled up his sleeves to show off his well-developed biceps.

I took my shirt off and draped it over my shoulders to use as a sweat barrier between my back and daypack. In the 1990s, expedition companies instructed Western women to wear skirts or long pants in Nepal, especially in the villages, and men were expected to keep their shirts on. By 2003, so many trekkers had ignored these dress codes that many trekking companies gave up requesting that their clients wear conservative clothing. In Katmandu, Westerners are seen wearing any and all styles of contemporary clothing, including halter and tank tops, short shorts, body piercings, and newly acquired Tibetan-lettered tattoos. Immodest Western dress may still offend some Nepalese, but Western women in shorts and men without shirts are no longer uncommon sights on the main trekking trails.

I mentioned previously Rinpoche Tenzing, the Lama of Tengboche, saying, "People should do what they want." Though it was in another context, after 2003, I decided to wear what I wanted in Katmandu and on the trail. In a village, if I feel like I am offending local sensibilities, I put my shirt on. But for the most part, my experience is that going shirtless only offends old-line caste-conscious Hindus in Katmandu. Some villagers and mountain people find it curious and odd, but not particularly offensive, that a man would choose to go shirtless. The high country is populated mostly by Buddhists, "Third Way" followers like the Rai, and animists. They are less uptight about personal dress than are conservative Hindus. The only time I was confronted in Asia for going shirtless was when I was jogging in New Delhi. An orthodox Hindu lectured me in a haughty tone, accusing me of being "unhealthy" by exposing my chest in public. I pointed out that Gandhi went shirtless, as do Hindu sadhus. He was not amused.

Trail Highs and Lows

I felt good. I was back to what had become my second home, hiking in the Himalayas. We were only in the foothills and hadn't yet had clear views of the great whitecaps, but it was a Himalayan trail. Sweat was trickling down my forehead, funneling along my eyebrows, and dripping off my face. My shirt was soaking wet and, even though my shirt was supposed to be a sweat barrier for my backpack, sweat had soaked into my daypack. But I was free. I had a week of Himalayan hiking ahead of me.

My soul sang. I would be enveloped by the gigantic night sky filled with stars so luminous and seemingly close enough to touch that a headlamp isn't needed to walk around camp at night. I would hear throughout the day and night the muted sound of a glacier-fed river rushing through the deep valley it cut into the great humped foothills. I would see in the distance the majestic peaks of the High Himalayas guarding the border with Tibet. I would be awakened in the morning by the gentle voice of a loyal kitchen boy bringing milk tea to my tent and then the humming of the cook in his kitchen as the powerful scent of a hot breakfast wafted through the campsite. My days would be filled with the glorious feeling of my legs powering up and down steep rocky trails while my lungs and heart pumped life through my body. These are the selfish reasons I keep coming back to the Himalayas.

Himalayan trails are not wilderness, because humanity has created the trails and villages are usually within a few hours' hike. But the wildness in one's soul can be released in a way that it can't in the midst of modern civilization. Not released like the Bacchanalia I experienced at the Tengboche Jubilee party, but released from all responsibilities other than putting one foot in front of the other. Within the greatest cathedral on planet Earth, the magnificent Himalayas, one feels such a powerful connectedness to Mother Nature. The feeling of sacredness combined with a free-spiritedness opens the mind and expands the soul in a way that has become a rare privilege for the modern urban dweller.

Trekking is an abnormal experience. For many, it's once in a lifetime. For a lucky few, it's an annual adventure. Removed from your ordinary life, you experience nature more intimately and appreciate its aesthetics more consciously and deeply. You notice and respond to the things you see, minute or gigantic, as beautiful works of art: the intricate articulated patterns of tree bark, the stunning colors of curvaceous flowers, and the awesome glaciated peaks.

That freedom and wildness of spirit coursed through my veins. And I could see and connect with my surroundings with a clarity and vividness beyond the normal. I was in love again.

Meanwhile, throughout the morning, Bill and Karen struggled up the trail. There were only a few descending sections as the trail continued to gain altitude and we hiked higher and higher. Bill and Karen needed to take frequent rest stops. Sanga and I reminded them of the need to hydrate, and they seemed to be drinking plenty of water, but they both looked flushed. Coping with the heat of the sun was causing them as much of a problem as the hiking. An old knee injury was beginning to bother Bill, and it was becoming obvious that Karen's hiking boots were not broken in and her feet were hurting. Neither Bill nor Karen complained, and both put on brave faces, but they were obviously challenged beyond what they had expected.

David also began to have problems. He was carrying a large expensive Nikon camera with a huge detachable lens. He had the serious shutterbug vest with multiple pockets for gear and attachments. David was positioning himself for a shot when he fell. The trail was slippery in spots from a soaking rain the previous night. David was so taken with the opportunity to use his photography gear that he fell again, and then again. The third fall was into a rocky stream, and he fell so hard, he was momentarily dazed and his arm severely bruised. It was very strange, because David seemed fit enough. But the altitude must have affected his balance, although we topped out at only around 7,000 feet in the morning. His excitement about photo ops must have made him a bit careless. But he handled the falls with self-deprecating humor, and seemed more concerned about denting his expensive lens than he was about his bruised arm.

Carl trod along at his own great galumphing pace, with a look of curiosity or contentment on his wise, kindly, and weathered face. He chuckled regularly at most anything anyone said that had the slightest bit of humor in it, and he sometimes chuckled without anyone saying anything. Carl looked like and said he was in a state of wonder and awe from the moment he landed at Tribhuvan Airport and first began to experience Nepal. He had taken seriously the advice, "Open your mind when you come to Nepal."

Dax, David (when he wasn't falling and hurting himself), and I hiked ahead of the group a few times. When we came to a fork in the trail, we would find a pleasant stream to sit beside or a boulder to sit on, and then wait for Sanga, Carl, Karen, and Bill to catch up. Sanga made sure to let the slowest hiker set the pace because he did not want the group to get separated.

Sanga, of course, was the only one who knew the trail. Because he didn't have a crew to help him make sure no one took a wrong turn, Sanga asked that we hike together. Typically, on a trek, the members can hike at their own chosen pace because the crew of porters, cook, kitchen boys, sirdars, and assistant sirdars are strung out along the trail. At a junction, each member can see someone or wait for someone who knows the correct trail. The sirdar usually assigns one member of the staff to be the "sweeper" and follow the last group member to make sure no one gets lost. The system is not perfect.

On the Langtang-Helambu trek in 2007, friend Jim got lost when the trail went through a village and there were multiple trails to choose from when he reached the other side of the village. He chose wrong and was only able to find our camp by paying a farmer two hundred rupees (less than $3) to lead him back to the trails' convergence and point him down the correct trail to our campsite. I have made the wrong choice at a trail junction many times, especially when I have been ahead of the group and thought I knew the route. But knowing a little Nepali, I can ask directions if I become insecure.

On my first trek in the Khumbu in 1995, three of us in the group came to a fork by a little waterfall somewhere north of Jorsale on the Base Camp Trail. Rather than wait for a crew member, we forged ahead, thinking we were still on the main trail that our sirdar, Nima, had told us to follow. About a mile past the waterfall, we heard a voice calling behind us. There was Nima running down the trail toward us. He had seen that our boot tracks went past the waterfall and missed the turn we were supposed to take. It amazed us that our sirdar was so vigilant that he knew our boot tracks and noticed we had missed a turn. There were many other tracks besides ours on that trail. Nima gave us a choice of backtracking or scramble climbing over the top of the little mountain the trail was skirting. We chose to scramble climb, and that was my first experience of climbing in the Himalayas. It was exhilarating and I wanted more. So getting lost led me to a new hobby—mountain climbing.

The rate of progress of our present group during the first morning was beginning to worry Sanga, Dax, and me. We finally hit a long descending stretch of trail down into a canyon and then a little up and there was a river valley spreading out below us, with the pretty village of Shivalaya, our planned lunch stop. But we would be eating lunch at two in the afternoon instead of noon as planned. Sanga had miscalculated the speed of our group by two hours for the first morning hike.

Dax and I pelted down the trail ahead of the others and then waited for them to catch up at a suspension bridge across from the village. Sanga led us over the bridge, which spanned a narrow stretch of the river Khimti Khola. (*Khola* is one of several Nepali words for river.) He led the group to a teahouse in the village. Since we didn't have a cook or crew yet, we ordered momos (dumplings) and dal bhat (the national dish of rice and lentils).

Sanga, Dax, and I huddled to discuss the plan for the afternoon and how long Sanga now thought it was going to take the group to get to Deorali, the village where we were supposed to spend the night. At the pace Bill and Karen were setting, Dax and I were afraid we would be hiking after dark to reach Deorali. I really did not want to hike on an unfamiliar trail after dark, and I was very concerned about how these first-time trekkers would handle a forced night hike the first day of the trek. Sanga, upbeat as ever, assured me the group would be able to handle it. He thought they would be able to pick up the pace after a meal and as they began to get their trail legs. But his main point was that, whether we had to hike in the dark or not, we had to get to Deorali that night. We had to stick to the schedule in order to arrive in Basa village with sufficient time to experience Basa and then hike back to Phaplu to catch our flight to Katmandu and not miss our return flights to the States.

I was less sanguine about the prospect of Bill and Karen increasing their hiking speed. It was beginning to look to me like Sanga had assumed the speed of our group would be that of experienced outdoorsmen, not that of an overweight lawyer and Southern belle who hadn't bothered to break in her hiking boots. Dax and I told Sanga we wanted to hike ahead with David, and that we should be able to get to Deorali before nightfall if we hiked hard and fast. Sanga could keep pace with Carl, Bill, and Karen and make sure they would be safe on the trail if they had to hike after dark. Sanga agreed and gave us directions on how to find Deorali.

While we wolfed down momos, dal bhat, tea, and Fanta Orange soda, Sanga and I presented the plan to the group. No one seemed particularly concerned that the group would be splitting up for the rest of the day. Perhaps the slower members felt some relief at not holding Dax and me back. But when we hiked out of Shivalaya, and Dax and I started hiking fast and hard, David hung back. He seemed unsure of whether he wanted to accompany Dax and me or stay with the others. His propensity for falling must have shaken his confidence, or maybe his bruised arm hurt enough he wanted to take it easy. So Dax and I clapped David on the back, told him we would see him in Deorali, and then started humping double-time up the trail.

Pushing Hard

We hiked as fast as we could, running when we had easy trail. I set the pace. Dax kept up with me but would start to whine if I pulled ahead. I was determined to reach Deorali before nightfall. So I pushed hard and barked at Dax to keep up or I'd leave him behind, it was up to him.

I felt very strong, perhaps to some extent relative to the slowness and tentativeness of the other members of the group. But I had conditioned well over the summer through daily workouts of bicycling, rollerblading, kayaking, and occasionally running.

The last time I had visited Dax in LA, he put me to shame on the treadmill in his gym and then in street running around his neighborhood. But during the summer, outdoor workouts, rather than gym training with free weights and machines, had toughened me. Outdoor workouts provide a better conditioning base for trekking and mountaineering than gym workouts. The former create a stronger spirit and willingness to handle physical stress more than the controlled conditions of machines in a fitness club. Outdoor tough is tougher than gym tough.

The blood pumping through my veins, my lungs sucking hard for air, and my heart pumping rapidly felt great. And all around me was the great outdoors in these lush hills and valleys of the Middle Himalayas. Pounding up or scampering down the trail, dancing across wood plank and log bridges over streams—it all felt good. My senses were tuned in and the physical and spiritual challenges were a relief from ordinary life in Indianapolis. When I thought we were getting close to the village, I pushed even harder and did leave Dax in my dust. I arrived around six in the evening, just as dusk was settling on the village.

Sanga had told us to go to the Highland Guest House on the right side of the stream bisecting the village, but when I got there, I was told there were no empty rooms. I was visibly upset. The didi who was in charge seemed to be ignoring me and my plight; she was talking animatedly with a young man. (*Didi* means elder sister, but women who run teahouses and lodges are called "Didi." Sherpa society is matriarchal in certain ways, and many women run Sherpa businesses.) The young man spoke English and explained to me that she was telling him a group of porters had come to the lodge just a little while ago and they were now at another lodge on the other side of the stream.

God, I hoped it was our crew! A bahini (little sister or young woman) led me out of the lodge and across a little stone bridge to the Sunshine Lodge.

It was magical. Our porters had arrived at the lodge before I did. They must have taken a shortcut to beat me to Deorali, because they did not pass me on the trail. They had hiked the day before from Phaplu to Deorali, spent the night in Deorali, and then left early in the morning to get to Jiri, pick up our duffels, and hike back to Deorali. Amazing! They had hiked double the distance I had that day, in less time.

A young-looking and handsome "Sherpa," Arjun Rai, was the assistant sirdar in charge of the crew. (The assistant sirdars are designated Sherpas by some Nepalese trekking companies, even though they are not of the Sherpa ethnic group. Westerners often incorrectly refer to porters, or anyone working on a trekking crew, as Sherpas.) I had not met Arjun before, but I was too tired and hungry for any long introductions to him or the crew at that point. I just thanked them all, shook hands with each, and then had them show me where they had put the duffels. The duffels were organized and stacked outside of rooms ready for our group, whenever the others arrived.

Dax arrived about fifteen minutes later, and immediately demanded food and drink. We were both very tired after trail running and humping hard for over three hours. But I said, "You know, we have to go back and find the others after we finish eating." Dax basically told me to stuff it, that he was not going to hike back down the trail in the dark. Sanga was with the group, and they didn't need us. He said that when he finished eating, he was going to bed. And he did.

After I finished eating and arranging my kit in a room with Dax, I headed back down the trail to find our group. The last stage of the trail into Deorali was weird. Deorali is built on a pass at about 9,000 feet. A stream runs down the middle of the village, and then spreads out and tapers off into a long shallow fall over the rocky trail leading up the incline into the village. The water is only a couple of inches deep, but it flows over the trail into the village, so your shoes get wet when you come to Deorali from the west. Mine got wet a second time as I hiked back out of Deorali.

About an hour outside the village, I found our group. I actually heard Carl's voice before I saw them. It was not totally dark, as there were stars out, but there was some cloud cover dimming the natural light of the Himalayan night. Carl was out front and I heard the encouraging tone in his voice as I approached.

They were three hours behind Dax and me. I had been in Deorali an hour before I hiked back down the trail; I hiked an hour to find them, and they had an hour's hike ahead of them. The group was taking six hours to hike from Shivalaya to Deorali, a hike that had taken Dax and me three hours.

People unfamiliar with Himalayan trekking always ask, "But how many miles is that?" Trail distances are not measured in miles or kilometers. No one takes such measurements. Distances are given in hours of walking time. So care must be taken in estimating walking time, because locals, seasoned trekkers, and novices walk at different rates. Our group was moving at about half the speed Sanga had assumed in his calculations for the revised trek plan.

The looks on Bill's, Karen's, and David's faces were a combination of fearful anxiety and fatigue. They looked like they were on a death march to Deorali. Sanga was bringing up the rear, and even he looked a little worried. Bill did not have a headlamp, so Sanga was shining his light on the trail for Bill to follow. I had an extra headlamp and loaned it to Bill. He threw his arm around my shoulder, leaning on me and heaving in gratitude and exhaustion.

I told them the lodge was only a half-hour up the trail. I lied. But their looks of relief were worth the demerit on my record with Saint Peter. David looked wide-eyed, like a lost child or shell-shocked soldier. Karen looked like she was about to cry. And Bill just looked totally gassed. Carl looked no different, and kept up an optimistic chatter obviously intended to buck up the spirits of the others. I assured them that Dax and I had checked into a lodge and warm food and beds awaited them.

As we straggled onward toward Deorali, I hung back and walked with Sanga for a bit. He whispered that the group was much slower than he thought they would be. He was especially worried about Bill. He did not think Bill could handle the pace we would have to keep up to reach Basa in time. He also thought Karen might not be able to handle it. I was even less optimistic. I didn't think any of them could handle it, except Dax. We walked into the lodge in Deorali about nine in the evening, three hours later than Sanga had expected.

11

MELTDOWN IN DEORALI

The friendly didi who ran the Sunshine Lodge in Deorali had large pots of milk tea awaiting our arrival. We dropped our backpacks and trekking poles in the corner of the dining room and slumped onto the cushioned benches. Carl and Karen leaned back against the wood-plank wall. Bill and David cradled their heads in their arms on the dining table. Sanga and a bahini bustled around our slouched bodies like hens with their chicks, pouring tea and taking food orders to relay to the didi who was in the kitchen preparing dinner for us. Sanga had resumed his chipper attitude and was joking around and laughing, trying to lift the flagging spirits of our group members.

Spirits did begin to rise as bellies began to fill with warm food, tea, and Fanta Orange . (I don't know the history and why it has developed, but this is the bottled soft drink sold at most lodges and teahouses in Solu Khumbu. It's the only soft drink available in many teahouses.) Dax strolled casually into the dining room and immediately began a nonstop commentary on and critique of the meager food selections at the Sunshine Lodge. Karen removed her hiking boots and was massaging her sore and blistered feet, but she was able to laugh at Dax's faux gourmet put-on. David quietly tended to his bruised arm and dented camera equipment.

Bill began to perk up and managed to raise himself from the cushioned bench to resume flirting with Karen. He chided her good-naturedly about her blistered feet and for not breaking in her new boots before coming to Nepal. Carl continued leaning against the wall, smiling contentedly and sipping milk tea.

Without any warning, Bill all of a sudden looked across the table at me and said, "Rasley, you son of a bitch, I ought to punch you in the face." He was smiling as he said it, but he didn't laugh or give any indication he was kidding. I asked what he meant, and he said, "For getting me into this." I tried not to lose my temper, especially since the group was beginning to recover from the trauma of their "death march" to Deorali, but I was pissed off and shot back at him, "What the fuck do you mean, getting you into this! You want to punch me in the face! Try it!" We glared at each other and then Karen interrupted us, "Come on, guys . . ." Neither of us wanted to upset Karen, or anyone else, so we both dropped it and returned our attention to the food on the table in front of us. But my anger toward Bill continued to simmer. I tried to ignore him and concentrate on eating and talking to Sanga, Carl, and Dax.

I would later understand that my eruption of anger at Bill over the dinner table was due in part to overexertion and altitude. But it was white hot at the time. I would also later regret the rift that developed between Bill and me. He had been a good friend for over thirty years. My inability to better handle irritation with Bill cost me his friendship. That was the greatest expense of my trek to Basa.

⊡ ⊞ ⊚ ⊡ ⊟

While we were eating, I overheard Bill telling Karen that he had decided to quit the trek and was going to return to Katmandu. He urged her to go with him. The dining room was small enough that no conversation was private, and the rest of the group could hear

Bill trying to convince Karen they should drop out of the trek and head back to Katmandu. Sanga and I exchanged glances, then he went over to Bill and Karen's side of the table, sat down, and began talking up what a great job the group had done on the first day and that the second day would be "not so hard." But Bill was adamant that he wanted to quit. Sanga asked him to please try hiking tomorrow morning and see how he felt. He explained that it would not be possible to return to Katmandu from Deorali, but that, if Bill still wanted to quit by lunchtime tomorrow, Sanga would assign a porter to Bill to accompany Bill at his own pace to Phaplu. It was obvious from Bill's expression that he was not happy with Sanga's proposal, and he asked Karen what she wanted to do. Karen said she wanted to sleep on it and that they should see how they were feeling in the morning.

As we finished eating, members of our group collected their packs and poles and began moving into the rooms the Didi had arranged for us. Dax and I had already put our duffels in one of the rooms on the second floor. We finished eating last, because we lingered awhile at the dining table to talk over the troubling condition of the rest of the group. When we went up to our room, we found Bill's duffel inside the door, his pack on my bed, and a tube of unidentifiable white cream squished in the middle of the floor as if someone had stepped on the tube, squirting a blob of the cream out on the floor.

Dax had a fit and started hooting and bellowing about crass Hoosiers squirting their "Hoosier cream" on the floor. I picked up Bill's pack and duffel, carried them down the hall, and deposited them in a room with David, who made no complaint. He was already in bed and still nursing his sore arm. Apparently, Bill was in the WC. I went back to our room, closed the plywood door, and latched the hook, locking out anymore contact with Bill or the others for the night, I thought. Dax continued to screech and squawk about Hoosier knaves and nincompoops. I burrowed

Meltdown in Deorali

down in my sleeping bag until I was warm and comfy and then giggled like a ten-year-old while Dax prated on about the hideous lack of manners that could only be attributable to Bill's Hoosier upbringing that he could leave that ghastly cream on the floor and not clean it up! Pointing out that Bill had lived in California longer than he had lived in Indiana did not deter Dax from his diatribe about the loutishness of Hoosiers—although he granted there were a few exceptions, and I might qualify on occasion.

Hypothermia

When Dax finally quieted down, I fell asleep but was awakened by a weak rapping on our door and Bill mewling my name. Grumpily, I unzipped my sleeping bag and unlatched the door, ready to be testy with him. Bill was standing there, ashen faced and shaking. He said, "Something's wrong with me." He explained that he was freezing and couldn't fall asleep. He was clearly in distress and was not joking. I put my arm around him and guided him back to his room, telling him I'd help him get comfortable and then get Sanga.

The possibility of hypothermia passed through my mind, but I dismissed it because I didn't think it likely he could be hypothermic after a hot meal and being in a warm bed. The outdoor temperature was around freezing and there was no heat in the rooms, so it was probably mid-forties Fahrenheit in Bill's room. But he should have been comfortably warm in the bed. Bill was not complaining of a headache, so I didn't think he had altitude sickness. I couldn't figure out what was wrong with him.

Then I saw his sleeping bag. Instead of an expedition-quality sleeping bag, Bill had brought a cloth bag like one would use for a backyard campout in Southern California. It probably had no rating, and certainly was not rated to zero Fahrenheit as recommended on Niru's gear list. Bill said he couldn't stop shaking, and it was no wonder. He had been trying to sleep in an unbuttoned flannel shirt and underwear in a cloth sleeping bag. No doubt his core temperature had dropped and he was mildly hypothermic. He was scared because he didn't understand what was happening to his body. I told him to button up his shirt and get in his bag. I zipped it up and started to pile on covers the lodge supplied, but he wanted to sit up. He said he felt a little nauseous and didn't want to lie down. So I draped the covers over him. I told him I would go find Sanga and come back. I started to turn off the light, but he asked me to leave it on. David groaned, rolled in his bed, and put a pillow over his head. Bill apologized to David, and I said I was sorry too and that I would find Sanga as quickly as I could.

I didn't know where Sanga was but assumed he was sleeping in the dining room. He wasn't there. I opened the door to the storeroom and shone my light around. There were Nepalese bodies scattered all over the floor, wrapped in rugs, blankets, or just huddled together for warmth. I shone my headlamp on faces, looking for Sanga. Men groaned and turned away from my light. Damn it! I didn't see him, and I was waking up all these tired porters. I whispered, "Sanga kahaa, Sanga kahaa?" (Where Sanga?) A young guy finally got up, answering in Nepali I didn't understand, but took me by the arm and led me back upstairs to the room adjacent to Bill's. I wanted to kick myself!

I woke up Sanga and we looked in on Bill. He was breathing rapidly and I was a little concerned about a possible heart attack. Sanga said no, that he was just mildly hypothermic. Sanga told Bill to put his jacket on over his shirt, wrapped him in two blankets and then zipped him into his sleeping bag. Sanga was clucking in Nepali about the inappropriateness of Bill's bag—at least that's what I think he was muttering about. Sanga told me to massage Bill's shoulders, arms, and chest while he went to get warm water. David groaned and rolled over again, trying to avoid the light. Bill and I both apologized to David, but Bill wanted to keep the light on. Sanga came back with a pitcher of warm water and asked Bill to drink slowly. Sanga told him to drink from it throughout the night.

When we were satisfied Bill had calmed down and was comfortable, Sanga told him we would leave but that his room was right next door and Bill should get him if he needed anything else. Bill wanted to keep the light on, but I pointed out that David needed to get some sleep. Bill apologized to all of us for the trouble and said to turn out the light, he'd be okay now.

Out in the hall, Sanga and I put our arms on each other's shoulders and shook our heads. I didn't know whether to curse or cry. It seemed like the expedition was cursed with one snafu after another. I needed sleep.

Each expedition has a "crux" day, but it usually comes midway or near the end, when the group is worn down from days of hiking at uncomfortably high altitudes. It was alarming that the group was struggling so badly the first day on the trail. I was no longer mad at Bill. I was worried about him. I felt bad about inviting him to join the expedition. Maybe he had some grounds for cursing me. But still, damn it, why had he not gotten in shape and why did he ignore Niru's gear list? For god's sake, he hadn't even brought an appropriate sleeping bag. Of course, he had not expected to have to hike at such a hard fast pace. We all thought this would be an introductory cultural trek, not an extremely difficult trek with twelve-hour hiking days.

My 2001 edition of Lonely Planet's *Trekking in the Nepal Himalaya* guidebook, which I carried with me on each trek from 2003, describes the trek from Jiri to Deorali as "a long, hard day" and if "you are not in good shape, you may have trouble" (pg. 192). We had trouble. The increase in altitude from Jiri to Deorali is approximately 900 meters (almost 3,000 feet), which is three times the recommended altitude gain for a trekking day. Three hundred meters or 1,000 feet is generally considered the maximum altitude a trekker should gain from one night to the next in order to avoid altitude sickness, and the trail has two long ascending stages that are especially tough for novice trekkers.

Sanga had not realized that, not only did we have a group of novice trekkers, two of our members were, as the guidebook says, "not in good shape." The group had been pushed to the edge of physical endurance, and we had gained enough altitude that we were all undoubtedly affected by it.

It was a dark night of the soul for me, wondering how the group could possibly cope with a week of hiking at the pace necessary to make it to Basa.

Dax rolled over on his side, and asked what was going on with Bill. I told him to go back to sleep. We'd talk about it in the morning. I needed to sleep.

SECOND DAY ON THE TRAIL: LOST ONE

꧁ꙮꙫꙭ꧂

Bill is usually gregarious, especially when sitting at table with food and drink, but at the breakfast table, he was quiet, as was the rest of the group. Only Sanga was not subdued. He was chirruping and doing his best to buck up the group's mood, while he helped the bahini serve the food.

On a trek, the sirdar is in charge of everything, so he oversees the food service, even when the group is eating in a teahouse or staying in a lodge. When a group is tent camping and eating in a meal tent, the sirdar directs the kitchen boys in serving the meals. He helps carry steaming pots of food from the cook's kitchen tent to the meal tent, where the trekkers sit around a table with tablecloth, napkins, plates, dishes, utensils, a full complement of condiments, and candles. The cook has some independence and status, because he has been trained and has a skilled position. But every sirdar I know worked as a cook before becoming a sirdar, so the sirdar knows the job and has authority over the cook if he chooses to exercise it. The English aristocrats who designed the form of trekking used throughout the Himalayas must have conceived of the sirdar's position as a combination of maître d', mule herder, and factory foreman.

We packed our duffels and daypacks, picked up our trekking poles, and were ready to begin the next long day of hiking. Sanga told us he was letting the porters sleep in because of the long days they had worked to get our duffels to us. Of course, he knew now how slowly our progress would be, so there was no need to send the porters down the trail ahead of the group, as is the normal practice. The porters would have no trouble catching this group, even though they were carrying the heavy loads of our duffels in their dokos, while we carried only light daypacks on our backs.

We walked out of the Sunshine Lodge into a clear morning. In Deorali, we were at about 9,000 feet so the air was crisper and not humid as it had been the day before when we hiked out of Jiri. It felt good to shoulder a pack and to get the arms and legs moving in the cool air, striding out of the village using trekking poles, clickety-click.

Trekking out of Deorali

We crossed over a wooden bridge, leaving Deorali behind, and were soon losing the altitude we had gained the day before. The descending trail was so steep that locals had cut steps out of rocks and boulders embedded in the hillside. The steep downward trail was more physically challenging than the ascending trail we hiked the day before out to Jiri.

A steep descending trail is hell on the quadriceps and hamstrings. And as those muscles and tendons tire, one begins to try to take more of the strain on the calf muscles until those muscles begin to sing with pain. Worst of all for aging feet, ankles, knees, and hips, on a steep descent the shock of each step down compresses the bones from the feet all the way up through the skeletal structure of the body. Our second morning was going to be even tougher than the first.

When I was a novice trekker, I thought using trekking poles was a bit fey—okay for Europeans, but not the thing for a manly American. On the first day of hiking my first Himalayan trail out of Lukla, I noticed that many trekkers bought walking staffs from stores or traders in Lukla or found them along the trail. Our sirdar, Nima Sherpa, told me to look for discarded staffs as we got an hour or so down the trail toward Phakding. And bless him, he was right. All along the trail were discarded walking sticks. Nima explained that a walking staff is extra weight, and after the novice trekker tires of carrying the extra weight, the staff gets ditched. His advice was to be strong enough not to need anything to hike a trail except your own legs.

I liked Nima's advice, but in 1996 during the Ladakh-Kanglachen expedition, I tried trekking poles for the first time. I didn't own any, but since the great John Roskelley used them, I decided they must not be too wussified. John let me borrow his a few times and showed me how to use them to take a little weight and compression off my legs with each stride. He told me to try to calculate how much less strain my legs would experience in a day of hiking if I reduced by a few ounces the impact of each step. I couldn't do the math, but he assured me it amounted to thousands of pounds of force over the course of a trek. I bought a pair before my next expedition in 1998 and have used them strategically on each trek since then.

Niru's gear list includes trekking poles, and I always recommend that all members of our groups bring trekking poles. All of the members of the current group had poles, except the one who would have benefited most from them. Once again, Bill had ignored Niru's list and my advice, and had not brought trekking poles. The first day, he used a stick he found by the trail as a walking staff. The second day, he purchased a staff with a bird figure as a handle. I hoped it was a phoenix and would help Bill rise from the dead. Perhaps a staff did reduce some impact on his sore knee, as he took the carved one home when he returned to California. But Bill would have been much better served with standard trekking poles, like the other members of the group brought.

The descending trail leveled off as we entered the village of Bhandar. The strain on our legs lessened and we were rewarded with the interesting visuals of chortens and a gompa (monastery). Village kids stopped us to make conversation and practice their English or just to ask for "ink pen." The kids we met in Bhandar had apparently been trained not to beg, which trekkers should appreciate. Sanga and I had warned our group members not to give kids money and to discourage children from begging, but to carry spare pens and pencils or other school supplies to give to kids we met in villages. Bhandar was an opportunity to show American beneficence, so we gave the kids we met some of our pens and pencils.

The Festival of Dasain

The ten-day festival of Dasain had begun, and many of the local people we passed in Bhandar and along the trail had their foreheads painted with elaborate tikas (called *tilaka* in India, but *tika* in Nepal). The celebratory tika in Nepal is usually a pink or red powder made with yoghurt and rice grains. Married Hindu women usually wear one red dot called a bindi, and sadhus and gurus may sport elaborate and colorful tikas, but during festivals many people of all faiths will decorate their foreheads with tikas.

Dasain is a Hindu religious festival but is celebrated by almost everyone in Nepal, like Christmas in the United States. The celebration is to commemorate Durga's triumph over evil forces, but it has become a family holiday. Nepalese who have left their villages return during Dasain to visit parents and the extended family back home. The main focus of the festival has become spending time with family and celebrating community.

The most interesting Dasain celebration I have experienced was at the ancient gompa in Kyanjin with Elliot and Briggie in 2004. We were invited by the caretaker monk to participate in the ceremony. The monks performed a chanting ceremony and played gongs and wind instruments, led by an aged monk with a long wispy white beard. The village women bustled around serving everyone who came to the ceremony hot chang (beer) from large iron kettles. It was quite impressive that the monks were able to maintain their chanting and playing as they drank cup after cup of hot chang. But what a wonderful religious ceremony—a Hindu festival celebrated in a Buddhist temple with everyone getting drunk and happy while monks chanted and played music. Not at all like the uptight, stiff-necked religious ceremonies common to many Christian churches. And a lot more fun!

Back on the Trail

East of Bhandar, the trail descended through tilled fields and crossed and recrossed a stream. We trucked over several log bridges. We walked through the little villages of Dokharpa and Baranda as we continued to lose altitude. The trail finally bottomed out at another river crossing over a steel bridge. Then it began to rise, which, perversely, was a relief. After a long descent when calf muscles have begun to scream, it feels good to be able to shift one's weight forward and put the strain more on the bigger muscles in the upper legs and thighs. But on a Himalayan trail, it will be a short-lived relief. It won't be long before the quad muscles are complaining about the now ascending trail.

We descended 1,200 meters (almost 4,000 feet) from Deorali to the river bottom by noon. But then we had to begin a long ascent to reach Kenja, our planned lunch stop. The hike from the valley floor up to Kenja required us to regain half the altitude we had just lost. Kenja's altitude is 5,249 feet (1,600 meters).

While I enjoyed the diversity of the terrain hiking through the Middle Himalayas in Solu, it was striking how much more up and down we encountered, as opposed to the generally ascending trails hiking north in the Khumbu or the primarily descending trails hiking south back down the Khumbu trails. I was surprised that the huge hills and valleys of the Middle Himalayas created such challenging hiking. I had incorrectly assumed that hiking the foothills would necessarily be easier than hiking in the High Himalayas. Of course, the much higher altitude in the Khumbu creates a tremendous challenge in itself, with which, thankfully, our group did not have to contend. The challenge of gaining and then losing 1,000 meters in less than half a day was more than enough for our group of novices.

Hiking up toward Kenja, we met more children on the trail. These kids were also polite, perhaps on their best behavior for

Children on the trail to Kenja

Dasain. We all enjoyed trying to converse with the kids, but Karen could not pass any child without trying to communicate and demonstrate her fondness for kids. She delighted in finding something special in each child we met on the trail.

I taught Karen how to ask a child's name and how to tell her name in Nepali: "Timro nam ke ho?" (What is your name?), "Mero nam Karen ho" (My name is Karen). She would have learned every child's name we met along the trail, if Sanga had not gently reminded her that we needed to push on.

But before we arrived in Kenja, we had to stop and play. Even Sanga agreed some fun time was justified. We met a young fellow who had built, no doubt with help, a swing along the side of the trail. It was constructed out of chopped-down tree limbs and rope. He offered to let each of us take a turn on the swing. It wasn't a money-making project; it was just for fun. Karen would have spent the rest of the day swinging and playing if our mother-hen sirdar had not gently scolded her, reminding her we must hike on to our lunch stop for needed nourishment.

Bill, however, was not having fun. Outside of Kenja, he unsuccessfully tried to rent a mule. He was not getting better trail legs, as Sanga had hoped. His pace wasn't slowing, but it wasn't improving and his knee was bothering him more than it had the first day.

Bill knew he couldn't hike fast enough to get to Basa within our time limits. Sanga, Bill, and I talked over what we could do that would still allow Bill the chance to have a positive experience. We had been in such a hurry I had not spent time with, or gotten to know, the porters. I was not happy about that, as I very much like to get to know every member of the crew. But, of course, Sanga knew all the guys well, as they were all from Basa or villages near Basa.

Sanga told us that one of the guys, Some Rai, was studying English and had volunteered to be Bill's porter-guide. Sanga assured us that, of the crew members we could afford to release, Some was the best for the job. Some, Bill, and Sanga planned a teahouse trek for Bill that would begin at Kenja and end at Phaplu. Some would carry Bill's duffel in his doko and allow Bill to set a pace comfortable for Bill. They would eat and sleep at teahouses and lodges. Sanga assured Bill he would have a private room each night. Sanga doled out enough rupees to Some to cover all of the expenses they would have for the teahouse trek, and gave Bill the ticket for the flight back to Katmandu from Phaplu. Sanga and Some calculated that Bill and Some would get to Phaplu a day or two before the rest of us were expected to arrive. So Bill would have the choice of flying out before the rest of the group or waiting for us, assuming we made it to Basa and back on schedule.

The porters separated Bill's duffel from the rest of the loads they were carrying. Some packed it onto his doko, and they were ready to go. Bill asked Karen once more if she was sure she didn't want to join him. She demurred. Karen did seem to be getting stronger on the trail, as Sanga had predicted.

Dax and I hugged Bill and wished him well. He seemed a little cold toward us, at least compared to the warm and gregarious Bill I had known as my friend. On reflection, "cold" wasn't how Bill seemed, so much as a little dead, like he had died a little or as if he wasn't all there. We trekked off, leaving Some and Bill behind us.

Trekking Reality

I have to confess a sin: I like to build myself up in my own mind and in others'. I want people to think I can do things others can't, that I have performed feats lesser humans cannot handle. This is a temptation I have faced, and I have sometimes succumbed to it. I shouldn't, because I've had a bellyful of that kind of posturing by litigators bloviating about how they kicked so-and-so's ass in a trial. Bill is the only other lawyer I've trekked with. I don't know that practicing law had anything to do with Bill's failure to condition properly for the trek or his failure to follow Niru's gear list. But lawyers do tend to think rather highly of themselves, so maybe he thought he was exempt from the rules that should be followed for a novice trekker to have a positive experience on the trail.

But I did not feel any triumph or superiority to Bill due to his inability to handle the trek. I felt a combination of sadness and anger—sadness for Bill that the trek had been so hard on him and on our friendship, and anger that he had made it harder on himself than it should have been. Bill had engaged in a strange exercise in self-sabotage before he left the States. Why would a highly intelligent person utterly disregard the gear list when packing for the expedition? Why did he not properly condition himself for the expedition after Dax and I had both stressed to him how important it was to get in shape? Lawyers may be overconfident, but they are supposed to pay attention to details and understand the importance of preparation for a trial. Bill had not prepared for a Himalayan trekking trial of his body, mind, and spirit.

I think it was a peculiar American hubris, a belief that he could do whatever he chose just because he wanted it. The movie *Field of Dreams* presents a uniquely American view in its theme of "build it and they will come." On one level, it is a naively beautiful view of reality: If you just believe in something strongly enough, it will come true. Such beliefs have powered building developments all across North America. It is a worldview in sharp contrast to the Buddhist attitude of acceptance of reality as it is. The American capitalist devotes himself to changing the environment to satisfy his desires. The Tibetan Buddhist devotes herself to adapting to the environment to enjoy it. Bill could not make the Himalayas adapt to him, and he didn't seem able to adapt to the Himalayas.

Five Hike On

I wanted to hike alone after Bill's departure. I felt the rupture of our friendship and mourned it. So I hurried ahead of the others, but as I passed the fifteen or so bhattis (teahouses) of Kenja and waved and chatted up kids I encountered, I wasn't paying attention to trail intersections. I was distracted thinking about Bill and missed the trail out of town. Then I became confused as to which direction I was supposed to go beyond Kenja. (Maybe the altitude was affecting me.) I soon realized I was lost. So I asked the next group of kids I saw which trail went to Sete, the site where we were to camp that night. The kids assured me I was on the correct trail and that I should keep going the same direction I was headed. I did and it ended at a farmer's field about a quarter mile out of town. When I passed those kids on my way back, they were laughing at me. I gave them the finger. They didn't know what it meant, but it made me feel better.

I discovered the trail was even steeper on the other side of Kenja. I caught up with the group and resumed my position out front with Dax. Carl was moving more easily on the trail and hiked with Dax and me much of the rest of the afternoon.

Surprisingly, David was struggling. I knew his arm was still hurting, but he was beginning to hike with a strange lilting gait. He said his groin was hurting, and he feared he'd pulled a muscle. He hadn't fallen all day, so that was an improvement, but he must have strained or pulled a muscle in one of his falls the first day.

Karen's feet were in pain. She was getting used to it, and was trying to grin and bear it. Her mistake of buying hiking boots and not properly breaking them in wasn't intentional, I learned. She explained that she had planned to break them in, but her business partnership had broken up a couple of months before our departure and dealing with that mess and opening a new office had required a great deal of time and energy. She had been unable to find the time to break in the boots or properly condition for extreme hiking. But she accepted the pain and trekked along with David.

Dax and I found our crew just before dark. They had passed us on the trail above Kenja and were now setting up camp outside of Sete on an overlook with an expansive view of a river valley and the 11,600-foot Lamjura Bhanjyang. Sete is nothing more than a couple of bhattis and a decrepit monastery.

The altitude gain in the afternoon hike from Kenja to Sete was equal to the altitude we had lost in the morning from Deorali to Kenja. The campsite was at 8,226 feet. Carl had thoughtfully brought an altimeter, so when we thought of it, we were able to take altitude readings. My trusty Lonely Planet guidebook provides altitude information for all the villages on the main trekking trails. For the first three days of the trek, it was useful because we were hiking the traditional trail from Jiri to Everest Base Camp.

This was the same trail Sir Edmund Hillary, Tenzing Norgay, and all the great mountaineers of yore had hiked to Mount Everest. Mountaineers like Norgay and Hillary hiked from Katmandu because construction of the road to Jiri didn't begin until 1963, ten years after the first summit of Everest. But since the airstrip was built in Lukla, it is unusual for any climbers or trekkers to commence their expeditions in Katmandu or Jiri. Hiking from Jiri to Lukla adds a week to the base camp trek. If the trek started in Katmandu, like Hillary's and Norgay's, another week of hiking would be added to get to Jiri from Katmandu. So most trekkers and climbers going up to the Khumbu opt for the one-hour flight to Lukla over the all-day bus ride to Jiri and then the weeklong hike to Lukla. Consequently, we met few trekkers on the trail.

We did meet a French group in the Sunshine Lodge in Deorali. They kept to themselves, aside from an animated conversation with Dax (who is fluent in French) about food. On the second day, we met a Swiss trekker and his guide who were hiking from Jiri on the traditional route to base camp up to the Khumbu. We crossed paths with them several times and enjoyed friendly exchanges. The Swiss gent was hearty and spry, and it was interesting to hear his comparisons of hiking in the Alps to Himalayan trekking. His guide was rather taciturn and, for the most part, stood apart when we stopped for rest and conversation on the trail.

David, Karen, and Carl arrived at the campsite near Sete after dark—again. David and Karen were hurting but put on brave faces. I hoped the first night of tent camping would agree with the group. And I was also hoping we would not be disappointed with our first meal cooked by Purna Rai. Purna and his kitchen boys had hiked from Phaplu to meet us at the campsite outside of Sete.

We were not disappointed. Purna, thankfully, was as good a cook as I have had on any expedition. He worked his magic in a makeshift kitchen in an outbuilding of the farm where we were camping. He must have known our group was in need of more than just a meal. He cooked up a feast of chicken, lamb, rice, potatoes, gravy, fruit, veggies, soup, chapatti, and rice pudding. Our first dinner cooked by Purna was not the ultimate feast of a celebration dinner for the last night of an expedition because it lacked a cake, but it was damn close.

We learned that Purna is the father of Arjun (our assistant sirdar). It was very sweet seeing the two of them working together. They didn't pay extra attention to each other, but there was obvious affection in the way they glanced at each other now and then as they worked to prepare and serve our food. They both smiled with pride when Sanga told us during dinner that they were father and son.

I slept that night in a North Face expedition tent on a bluff across a deep valley from the Lamjura Danda, the 11,600-foot mountain ridge we would have to cross the next day. It felt better to be sleeping in a tent, although my trepidation about the group's ability to handle the first high pass tomorrow was scratching at my consciousness.

Another troubling thought flickering through my weary mind was instigated by my earlier musings about American developers and their *Field of Dreams* attitude of "build it and they will come." Was Niru's dream for Basa village in the same category?

Niru wants to bring modern education to the kids in Basa. He also dreams of making Basa a tourist destination. And he wants to bring electricity and piped water to Basa. His dream is to make

Basa like the tourist villages of the Khumbu. By completing the school and bringing the first tourists to Basa, are we not starting Basa down the same road the Khumbu Sherpas have followed? Is Niru's vision for Basa the same sort of vision as that of Western developers when they look at a small farming town outside a major metropolis and see a shopping mall or housing development?

I had to put that thought away for the time being. It was challenging enough to wonder how our group would handle the Lamjura pass in the morning. Anyway, restorative sleep had to take precedence over worries about what tomorrow would bring for our group and the future of Basa village.

13

THIRD DAY ON THE TRAIL:
MORNING IN THE SHADOW
OF LAMJURA DANDA

Finally, a day began like it's supposed to on a trek. Kumar Rai and Rudra Rai awakened me by gently calling at my tent flap, "Good morning, sir. Tea, sir." Instead of waking up in a short narrow bed inside a small room with plywood walls, I woke up in the little yellow capsule world of an expedition tent. All of my worldly possessions for life on the trek were secure inside the yellow capsule and I was tucked comfortably in my Gander Mountain sleeping bag. Two of the "kitchen boys" brought hot dudh chiyaa (milk tea) to each of the tents. Kumar held the tin cup, while Rudra poured tea, or coffee if preferred, with or without dudh or chini (sugar) to the specifications of each member of the group.

I shoved my backpack behind me to support my back while half sitting, and carefully took hold of the handle of the tin cup of tea Kumar handed to me; his tough hands were impervious to the extreme heat of the cup. I blew on the tea to cool it down and then leaned back, still in my sleeping bag up to my chest, inhaling the cool morning air combined with the rich scent of the milk tea. Ten minutes later, Pancha Rai and Nirman Rai, the other two kitchen boys, made their rounds to our tents, placing large steel bowls of taato pani (warm water) at each of our tents, saying softly, "Taato pani, washing water." I finished off the cup of tea, pulled off my long underwear shirt, and splashed my face, neck, chest, and armpits with the warm water. I shook the water off like a dog and then quickly dried off with my quick-dry camp towel. There was a slight chill in the air. My mom would call it "brisk." I dressed quickly.

It wouldn't be cold enough at the altitude we would be hiking today to need long johns, so I pulled off my long underwear and put on trekking shorts and a t-shirt. Over those clothes, I put on wind pants and a long-sleeved pullover. Later in the day, as the temperature increased, I would be able to remove clothing and stuff it in my backpack. I slipped on sandals and went to the clothesline to retrieve my thermal socks. The socks, although worn the day before, felt dry and almost fresh from spending the night and early morning outdoors. Back in the tent, I pulled them on, shoved my feet into my hiking boots, and pulled on my light Gortex jacket. Outside again, I brushed my teeth, looking up at the imposing view of Lamjura Danda, which we would have to hike over before the end of the day.

Lamjura Danda is the name of one of several ridges, or mini ranges, that run north-south through the Middle Himalayas in Solu. Lamjura Bhanjyang is the Nepali name of the top of the ridge, where the trail crosses or passes over the Danda, which we would have to manage later that day. *La* is the Tibetan term for "pass." Tibetan terms and names are commonly used in the Himalayas by locals and foreigners on the Nepalese and Indian side of the mountains, as well as on the Tibetan side. Maps and guidebooks refer to the pass over Lamjura Danda interchangeably as Lamjura La and Lamjura Bhanjyang.

The other group members emerged from their tents, attending to their toiletries and dressing. After we were up and dressed, it would be time to repack our duffels. The porters stood around, trying not to look like they wanted us to hurry, but I knew they did. They couldn't tear down the tents and load their dokos until we were out of the tents and had repacked our duffels.

Sanga and Arjun came out of the kitchen shelter, calling to us, "Breakfast ready! Breakfast ready!" We hurried to finish cleaning out the tents and packing our clothes and personal kits back into our duffels. As soon as the duffels were zipped, porters hustled around, grabbing up duffels and shaking and shaping them to fit into the dokos. Other porters began tearing down tents. Like a well-oiled machine, the porters struck camp and organized their loads for the day.

While the porters were packing, I noticed the farmer who owned the field where we were camped milking a cow. Arjun saw me watching, came over, and said with a smile, "Fresh milk." "For us?" I asked. "For you, yes," Arjun replied with a broad grin.

Sanga pointed out a jug of warm water on a stand outside the meal tent. There was a bar of soap in a soap dish and a hand towel hanging from the water stand. Motherly Sanga encouraged us to wash our hands before breakfast. He stood by the meal tent, holding open the flap for each of us to duck inside. The kitchen boys had already set the breakfast table. On a clean but faded flower-print tablecloth were complete table settings arranged for the five of us, as well as a large basket of warm toast, jars of strawberry and grape jelly, marmalade, butter, and honey.

As soon as we were seated, Sanga, Arjun, Kumar, and Rudra began pouring tea, coffee, or hot chocolate into tin cups at each member's request, passing around toast, and bringing pancakes and omelets for our plates. They also spooned muesli, cereal and milk, and canned peaches, whichever we wanted, or any combination, into bowls for us. While we were eating, Arjun and Sanga filled our water bottles with boiled water. Wearing the traditional Nepalese topi hat, Purna poked his head through the tent flap, an inquiring look on his face. Between mouthfuls of food, we heaped praises on him for his efforts.

Our hunger sated and bulked up on calories, we were ready to start the day's hike. We hoisted ourselves off the metal folding chairs in the meal tent and picked up our water bottles from the end of the breakfast table. As we shouldered our packs, stretched, and picked up our trekking poles, the farmer's daughter and little son came over to say "Namaste!" and "Good-bye."

Manis, Chortens, and Prayer Flags

But all was not well with all members of our group. The pain in David's groin had spread into his right thigh. He described it as a stabbing pain. Ibuprofen during the night had not relieved the pain. Karen gave David some muscle-relaxing cream, which he applied before we started hiking. He reported that the cream spread warmth through his thigh and it felt better. We were closer to Phaplu than Jiri, so the best option for David was to keep hiking with the group. A short distance down the trail, however, it was obvious he was experiencing pain again. He didn't complain, but he walked with an awkward straight-legged gait, trying to keep tension off his upper right leg. At times he tried using one trekking pole like a cane, and at other times he tried to use both poles like crutches. David was moving more slowly than Karen, about as slow as Bill had been—definitely too slow for us to reach Basa within the time our schedule allowed.

Of course, there is no good day to be in pain and have difficulty hiking during a trek. But David may have chosen, or bad karma chose for him, the worst day. Ahead of us rose Lamjura Bhanjyang, about 11,600 feet high. The trail rises nearly 4,200 feet from Sete to the top of the pass, and then descends about 4,000 feet on the other side of the La. Our campsite was on the other side of the pass. This would be a very challenging hike under any circumstances even for experienced trekkers and climbers. Four-thousand feet up and down in one climbing day is the most altitude gain and loss I had experienced on a Himalayan climb. Of course, climbing at high altitude is much more demanding than the trekking we were doing, but still, an excess of 8,000 feet gain plus loss is a very challenging day on the trail. The day of the Lamjura La was far more difficult than my novice trekker friends had bargained for in signing up for an introductory cultural trek.

During breakfast, Sanga told us that there would be several ups and downs before the steep trail up to the top of the pass and then a very steep descent on the other side. He had downplayed the amount of altitude we would gain and lose. But it made me cringe to think about how David was going to handle the steepest stages of the trail, both ascending and descending.

We settled into a slow but steady rhythm, however, following the porters toward the looming Lamjura Bhanjyang. The hike was beautiful. We neither passed through nor saw any villages the entire morning. We hiked by a few goths (not the opponents of ancient Rome nor teenagers wearing black eye shadow; "goth" is the Nepali term for a herder's shelter) and a few farm settlements. A couple of the farmers had constructed bhattis as additions to their homes.

Because the land was less rocky and more fertile, the farms we hiked past were larger than the little terraced plots I was used to seeing in the Khumbu. We hiked through rhododendron, pine, and birch forests. Moss hung from the low branches of trees. It was as if we had been magically transported to the low country of the Carolinas or Georgia in the southeastern United States, except our altitude was higher. Birds called in the forest. I'm not a birder, but my Lonely Planet guidebook claims there are more than 800 species of birds in Nepal and hiking this stage of the trail offers the best birding in Nepal, with colorful sunbirds, minavets, flycatchers, tits, and laughing thrushes hanging out below Lamjura Bhanjyang.

Third Day on the Trail

Carl and Sanga passing by mani stones

Dax and David with kids by chorten

We finally broke out of the forested hillsides to begin the steep ascent up to the pass. A circle of mani stones with Tibetan prayers carved and painted on them created a little roundabout on the trail. It is customary for Buddhists to walk around mani stones and prayer flag poles on the left side, touching them with the right hand and chanting "Om mani padme hum." Just as Buddhist prayer wheels are spun clockwise, the way the wheel of life turns, so we are to pass round sacred places.

Mani stones and Buddhist prayer flags along the trail and in the settlements indicated that Sherpas, who are Tibetan Buddhists, are the dominant ethnic group in this area. Except for the lack of great white-capped peaks and the greater size of the farms, this stage of the trail felt much like trekking through the Khumbu on the Base Camp Trail. Correction, it had a similar feel to the Base Camp Trail before the development of the many lodges that now cluster around every settlement between Lukla and base camp. The trail from Sete to Lamjura La was steep and rocky and the only inhabitants we encountered were Sherpas.

Mani stones for Tibetan Buddhists, like the Sherpas, have a similar purpose to crosses erected along highways in the United States. Local people commission stone masons to chisel sacred sayings or mantras on stones to commemorate significant events, such as the death of a parent, child, or spouse, or the birth of a child after a difficult pregnancy. The most common "prayer" the Sherpas use on mani stones is "Om mani padme hum." It is Tibetan and has different translations. One I have heard is "Buddha is the perfect lotus flower." Another is "Praise the jewel in the lotus." But the literal meaning is not as important as the sentiment of praising the perfection represented by Buddha and engaging in the practice of meditative chanting.

If the stones are arranged to create a circular structure or it is a solid structure made of poured cement, which looks like a little temple with no entrance or interior, the structure is called a chorten. (A stupa has a similar exterior form, but is larger and has an entrance, so one can enter and worship within the stupa.) Most Sherpa settlements have chatdars in the center of the settlement, which are tall wooden poles with prayer flags attached. Tibetan Buddhists believe that each time the wind blows and flaps the flag, the prayer dyed on the flag is "said." It is a much more efficient and economical way of ensuring that prayers are said for oneself, family, village, or all of humanity than the method used by medieval Christian noblemen, for example. The latter would leave a great sum of money to an order of monks to build a chantry and to pray in perpetuity for the soul of the departed. Tibetan Buddhists only have to bear the cost of erecting the pole, purchasing the flags from monks, and occasionally replacing a torn prayer flag. Perhaps the Christian monks found a sharper financial angle for making money off rich noblemen for their orders. But many Buddhist gompas are still thriving in Nepal, while there aren't too many thriving medieval Christian monkish orders.

Lunch by a Kharka

We finally stopped for lunch at one of the few settlements on the trail. The farm family that built the settlement had added a little bhatti with kitchen facilities in the form of an outbuilding or shed, which Purna could use to cook our lunch. The trail ran right through the settlement, which was to the side of a pretty kharka surrounded by hills on the approach to Lamjura La. Nepalese mountain people have common grazing pastures, called kharkas. Grassy land usable for grazing cattle or sheep is at a premium in the high country, so pastureland is generally not owned by individuals or families. Traditionally, English sheepherders were allowed to graze their sheep on common land in villages ("the commons"), and American cattlemen were allowed to herd and graze their stock even on private land, which was left open for cattle drives. But one of the features of the development of modern capitalism in the West has been the division of land into fenced off properties and the loss of common spaces for grazing animals. In Nepal, however, common grazing land is still the norm. Modern capitalism has begun to affect the economy and culture of Nepal, but the Hindu-Buddhist respect for life, and especially other mammals, seems to promote cooperation among farmers, herders, and the larger community. Cows, monkeys, and dogs walk freely around the busy streets and temples of Katmandu. And in all the areas of the high country in Nepal I have visited, the tradition of maintaining free and open kharkas is preserved.

We played with our host's kids while we waited for Purna to prepare lunch. The children were fascinated with the colossal size of Carl's hiking boots and the length of his trekking poles. Carl let the kids run around with the poles. They tried to mimic a trekker hiking with poles. I noted with interest that these kids, who do not have access to TV, movies, or video games, did not pretend the poles were guns or javelins, as I would expect of American kids.

It was only a short wait for lunch because Purna and the kitchen boys had arrived at the settlement before we did, even though we started down the trail after breakfast while they cleaned up and tore down the kitchen at Sete. They had passed us on the trail. Our porters had also arrived at the settlement before we did, and they were enjoying a break inside the bhatti while we ate lunch outdoors.

A typical feature of Himalayan settlements along trekking trails is the communal charpi (toilet). The locals had no need of such an amenity. Instead of collecting human excrement in a central place and then having the problem of what to do with it, the mountain people used their dung for fertilizer and peed anywhere except in a water source. But they learned that Westerners expected a private place for such affairs. Charpis in rough settlements with few tourists hiking through are quite Spartan. They are usually a clapboard structure with a hole in the floor built over a hillside. Sometimes there is straw provided and sometimes toilet paper. Charpis in villages where more trekkers are expected are likely to have a bucket of water with a little pitcher floating in the bucket. The lodges, which have been built in the last ten to fifteen years in response to the government's encouragement of the trekking-tourist industry, have running water.

Expedition companies usually provide toilet paper for clients but encourage members to bring their own roll to carry on the trail. Nepalese paper (usually pink in color, for some reason unknown to me) is rather rough on the more sensitive Western butt, so one might appreciate that little comfort of one's own TP roll from home when doing business in a nasty charpi in a rough settlement along the trail. I prefer to avoid nasty charpis, whenever feasible, and to enjoy more natural spots behind boulders or trees.

Some companies, like Adventure GeoTreks, include a toilet tent with the common gear. A toilet tent is at least six feet in height, but only about two feet wide and two feet deep. The tent has a zipper from bottom to top on one side for an entrance. The toilet tent is erected over a hole dug in the campground by one of the kitchen boys. Inside the tent is a toilet seat set on folding legs. Trekkers are encouraged to burn (carefully) used toilet paper. When the porters and kitchen boys break camp, the hole is filled.

It's always an amusing sight to see the toilet seat passing on the trail on the back of one of the kitchen boys. But one thing about crapping in the Himalayas is that, whether you're gripping a boulder or standing in a nasty old charpi, the view will help bring satisfaction.

After finishing lunch, it was time to hike on. David struggled to his feet and crutched off, with Karen following, trying to walk gingerly on her ripped up feet. The Lamjura La awaited us.

Portable toilet and meal table on porter's back

Room with a view: trail toilet (charpi)

Third Day on the Trail

14

OVER THE LA: KAREN IS NARAYANI

Hiking up to the top of the Lamjura La was difficult for all of us. It was hell for David. Having to lean forward and lift his feet up step after upward step, he could not maintain the straight-legged gait he had adopted on easier terrain. He later told me it felt like a knife stab in the thigh with each step. The relief he'd gotten

At the top of the pass: prayer flags on Lamajura La

from Karen's muscle-relaxing cream had worn off long before we reached the steepest stretch of the hike up to the pass. But he gutted it out, accepting the pain without complaint.

When we finally reached the top of the pass, we were inside a cloud. The temperature had dropped considerably, which had made the difficult ascent somewhat more bearable. We had stripped off our jackets and pullovers earlier in the day but had need of the warmer clothing again as our altitude increased and the clouds that enveloped us hid the sun.

We earned a rest and gratefully sprawled about, stretching aching legs. Mani stones were strewn all around a series of little humps or hillocks sprouting around the top of Lamjura La. Typical of a high Himalayan pass, prayer flags strung from poles and boulders flapped in the wind.

Lamjura La is the highest point on the traditional Base Camp Trail from Jiri to Namche Bazaar. Namche is well up the Base Camp Trail north of Lukla, far north of our trek to Basa. So we were definitely high, even though we were in the Middle Himalayas. Niru had told us we would be able to see Mount Everest at the top of the pass if it was a clear day. Unfortunately, there were no magnificent photo ops because we were inside a cloud.

Our porters and kitchen crew passed us while we rested on the La. We watched as they moved slowly and carefully over the pass and disappeared from view as the cloud enveloped them on the other side of the ridge. It was time for us to descend too. As we stuffed snack wrappers in our pockets, took a slug from water bottles, and then hoisted packs, Sanga bustled about checking on each member of the group and offering encouragement for the long descent in front of us.

The fog made the descent a bit more perilous with less visibility. I was especially concerned about David, given his propensity for falling. But he was moving slowly and carefully using his poles like crutches.

I wondered how Bill was doing.

Karen, like David, was in increasing pain. The first stage of the descent was very steep and rocky, which put so much pressure on her blistered feet that, despite the moleskin she'd taped over the sore spots on her feet, blisters were tearing off inside her boots and socks. The trail became less difficult as it snaked through another fir and rhododendron forest. After descending 4,000 feet, the trail finally leveled out into another river valley. We crossed the river by a wood bridge and then recrossed it on another bridge with a series of stone steps leading up to the bridge. On the second bridge, a lone bovine joined us.

In the Himalayas, it is common to share trails with cattle. They walk the trails more surefooted than most novice trekkers. In the High Himalayas, the first time a thousand-pound yak ambles up and joins you walking a rocky trail and then over a swinging cable bridge is a bit startling.

The yak is shaggy-haired, long-horned, and male. Females are called naks, but it is common to refer to either sex as yak. Yaks live at high altitudes in the Khumbu and are not seen in the Middle Himalayas, so the bovines we met on the trail to Basa were water buffalo, ordinary cows and steers, and dzopkyo or dzo (a yak-cow hybrid).

One lesson important for the novice trekker to learn is to move to the high side of the trail whenever crossing paths with cattle. If you move to the side of the trail on which there is a drop-off, a push or bump by a steer could send you tumbling down a hillside.

Our bovine companion hung out with us along the trail for a while but left us before our route turned south at the village of Junbesi on the Junbesi Khola (Junbesi River). At this point, we left the old Base Camp Trail, which continues east and eventually turns north to Lukla. The trails we would hike from Junbesi to Basa were essentially "locals only," because there are no trekking or tourist destinations on the trail to Basa. My Lonely Planet guidebook was of no further use, because, other than describing hikes around Phaplu, it doesn't mention Basa or the Basa Valley area.

The day was waning. When we turned off the old Base Camp Trail, Sanga told us that the campsite was not far. He said we would follow the trail along the Junbesi Khola, and that our campsite was at a settlement called Beni, downriver from Junbesi.

Our porters and kitchen crew were ahead of us, so I decided it would be safe to hike at my own speed the rest of the way to the campsite. Since it was supposed to be on the river, I couldn't get lost as long as I tracked the river. I picked up the pace and left the group behind.

At the next river crossing, the largest herd of sheep I had ever seen in Nepal held me up. Sheep are not herded in the High Himalayas, so I had encountered few herds of sheep and was surprised to see a few shepherds coaxing hundreds of sheep across the river with shouts and the occasional encouragement of a stick to the rump.

When the sheep turned off the trail and I was able to pick up the pace again, a filmy rain began to fall. It was not raining hard enough for me to go to the bother of dropping my pack to get out rain gear. But the sun was rapidly going down behind the Lamjura Danda, now west of us. So I kept up a fast hiking pace to stay warm.

I passed through a settlement just off the river. I was beginning to tire and was getting frustrated that I hadn't found the campsite. I saw a second settlement off the main trail and up a steep side trail. I thought our campsite might be up there, because it seemed like I had already hiked farther than where I had expected to find the campsite, based on Sanga's directions. I hiked up the trail, which became so steep the locals had cut steps into stone on the hillside. At the top of the hill was a beautifully appointed lodge built out of logs, but no campsite. I hiked back down and waited for the group. The sun had gone down, but I saw their headlamps bobbing along the trail after about a fifteen-minute wait. As they approached, the rain increased, so I got my rain poncho out of my pack and put it on.

Dax was freaking out. He had misplaced his headlamp and was having a fit about hiking in the rain and darkness. Without so much as a hello to me, he threw down his backpack and demanded that David and I shine our lights in it so he could look for his headlamp. We were all tired and upset that the hike had once again taken us so long that we were hiking after dark, but Dax was losing it. He calmed down after he found his headlamp. Out of my own frustration, I yelled at him and told him to quit acting like a baby. Sanga looked upset, and I'm sure he felt like the wheels were coming off, but he had the advantage of knowing exactly where the camp was, while we did not, and again, it had taken us much longer to reach the camp than Sanga had calculated.

Forty-five minutes of hiking further along the river and we finally reached the campsite. When we found it, the porters were setting up our tents. The kitchen and meal tents were already set up. Purna had hot tea waiting for us. We only had to stand around in the rain and darkness for a few minutes before the tents were up and dinner was ready to be served.

As soon as we were seated at the table in the meal tent, Sanga and Arjun were dishing out another of Purna's grand feasts and spirits began to rise. When their roles changed from worried guides to maître d' and chief server, Sanga and Arjun became all smiles and told jokes to cheer up the group. It worked. Karen seemed to enjoy showing off her incredibly blistered feet. They were beyond repair with moleskin, so she wrapped both feet in duct tape. She was actually laughing and joking while she ripped off bloody moleskin and taped up her feet.

Transformation

Karen had changed, in more ways than just getting blistered feet. At first, she was unsure of herself and had hung out with Bill for comfort and solidarity in insecurity. Karen confessed at the meal table that before the night in Sete she had not slept in a tent by herself. Not only had she not trekked before, she had not even done any long-distance hiking. She told us that, despite her lack of trekking experience, she felt connected to Nepal by reading about its culture and Tibetan Buddhism. Her sister spiritual seekers had encouraged her to cross the ocean and experience Nepal firsthand.

With the feeling that Nepal was calling her on a spiritual level, Karen told us that she thought she would be able to handle whatever the mountains had to give her. She had expected her friend, George, to accompany her on the trek. When he dropped out, it would have been easy for Karen to close off the possibility of Nepal for herself as well. She considered canceling with George, but the pull of Nepal was strong enough that she decided she had to give it a go.

When Karen had revealed that she hadn't broken in her hiking boots or trained for the trek, my first reaction had been that she too was suffering from American hubris in believing she could just hike the Himalayas without proper footwear or conditioning. But I had learned different from trekking with Karen for a few days. She was slow on the trail and her feet were killing her. But she had come to realize that by concentrating on the beauty around her and accepting that she had to put one foot in front of the other, the pain was just part of the process. Karen was gaining strength and earning her spiritual nickname, Narayani, powerful mother goddess and daughter of the Himalayas. Nepal and the mountains were giving to her, and she was accepting the gift.

15

FOURTH DAY ON THE TRAIL:
LOST TWO MORE

Ibuprofen and muscle-relaxing cream had done little for David during the hike to Beni. The next morning when he got out of his sleeping bag, the pain was even worse and spreading farther down his thigh. At the meal table, we talked over what to do, but there was really only one option, as Sanga had already pointed out the day before. David had to make the hike to Phaplu; from there, he could fly back to Katmandu.

Sanga informed us that the hike to Phaplu from Beni would only take a few hours and we should be there by midmorning, even at David's slow pace. For the first time, Sanga correctly calculated our rate of progress.

The hike due south to Phaplu was the easiest stage of the trek. We crossed another river, Chiyang Khola, by a cable and wood plank bridge, then hiked across a broad river valley before ascending and descending a rocky ridge.

Slipping and sliding over the ledge of the ridge and then down the steep rocky trail was intensely painful for David. But David, like Karen, was being transformed by his experience in the Himalayas.

On the first day, hiking out of Jiri, he had been careless and clumsy, falling repeatedly in his enthusiasm to photograph everything he saw. He was starry-eyed, and his balance was probably affected by the rapid increase in altitude. On the trail to Phaplu, he hiked with a grim determination. It was not that he had lost his eye for the wondrous beauty that surrounded him or his enthusiasm to be in this place. He still stopped to take the occasional photograph, but with his little digital camera rather than the big bulky Nikon he carried the first day. He was still an engaging companion, grinned between grimaces of pain, and did not complain at all about his physical suffering. David's transformation, in my mind, was that he became stronger through his willingness to accept the physical pain and to put one foot in front of the other despite the pain.

This seems a small thing, perhaps, to those who have not endured pain while hiking for miles and days. But I know what it is like to have to keep moving down the trail when it would feel so much better to stop and hire a pack animal or porter to carry you out, or to contract for a helicopter evacuation. I don't think David seriously considered those possibilities, although he may have fantasized about being flown out. Instead, he became more like my description of what is so attractive about the people of the High Himalayas; he became stronger and gentler.

The first time I hiked to Everest Base Camp in 1998, I began suffering from acute mountain sickness two days below Base Camp. The symptoms were not debilitating at first, severe headaches at night and feeling a little nauseous and weak in the morning. By the time we reached Gorak Shep, the last campsite below base camp, however, I was so weak I needed help to stand up. But I was determined to see Base Camp. I forced myself to put one foot in front of the other. A few hours later, I sat on a ridge looking down at my goal: Everest Base Camp. Then I hiked twelve hours to the medical clinic in Pheriche. It was very grim. I could barely stand. I had seen sick climbers being carried down the trail in dokos. I was determined not to rely on someone else to get me out of the predicament into which I had put myself. Looking back on it, I don't know where the strength came from to keep putting one foot in front of the other, but I found it.

David exhibited the same grit. He did it without kvetching and maintained a smile and pleasant disposition despite being in severe pain for three days on the trail.

In the lives that privileged professionals like David and me live in the United States, accepting physical pain is abnormal. If pain is experienced, we have a cornucopia of medications for relief as well as being able to turn to health-care professionals. Our culture encourages us to avoid pain. We are not to accept pain or discomfort; rather, we are encouraged to seek immediate relief. Most Americans would surely think it perverse and masochistic simply to accept pain and to continue to enjoy and appreciate the world around us rather than focusing our attention on escaping the discomfort of physical suffering. But that is how mountain people live, and that is how one from the West, like David, may choose to adapt to the experience offered. And he did.

The Village of Phaplu

A mule train passed us before we arrived in Phaplu. And, hooray, everyone in our group moved to the mountain side of the trail as instructed!

As we neared Phaplu, the trail widened and became dusty. It's a good idea to hike with a handkerchief around your neck or in a handy place, so if the trail gets dusty, you can cover your nose and mouth . You may look like a bandito with a handkerchief tied around your face, but better to look like a Wild West bandit than to breathe dust.

As we closed in on the village, local people hurried past us and children played along the trail. It was slightly disorienting to see people; we had seen so few on the trail in the last two days.

We followed Sanga down the main drag of the village, looking for the Number Lodge. Number is the name of the highest mountain visible from Phaplu. Shops, lodges, restaurants, and homes lined both sides of the trail. We hiked by the airstrip and a hospital. Phaplu looked to be a very prosperous Sherpa village. Many of the buildings were multistoried, which was in sharp contrast to the rough settlements we had passed through on the trail from Jiri.

Sanga has come through Phaplu on his way home to Basa village many times and has friends there. Sirdars make a point of developing contacts along the trails on which they guide clients. They use their contacts to find the best buys for local food, campsites, and lodges. But this was the first time Sanga had brought clients to Phaplu. He told me he knew the family that owned the Number Lodge and trusted them to look after David. This was also the lodge to which he had instructed Some to bring Bill when they arrived in Phaplu.

Sanga took care of making the arrangements for a room for David with the lodge didi. The group members rested and drank tea and Fantas in a little courtyard within the lodge. Our porters also took the opportunity for a rest, but the kitchen staff had hiked on ahead as we needed to continue to make time and the plan was that we would eat lunch farther down the trail.

After making room arrangements for David, Sanga gave him his Nepal Airlines ticket for return to Katmandu. He explained that David would have to buy a new ticket if he decided to fly before the scheduled date on the ticket, but Niru would arrange for a refund back in Katmandu. Otherwise, David could await our return from Basa and fly back with the rest of us. Sanga had given the same information to Bill.

We needed to say our good-byes to David and get on down the trail. Dax started to complain about the group always being in a hurry. He said he was tired of pushing the pace and would enjoy just hanging out in Phaplu for a while. This was disturbing and put Sanga in a difficult position because sirdars do not like to deny a client's request. So I said that, if he really wanted to hang out in Phaplu, he could stay with David, but the rest of the group needed to move on.

Dax actually considered the prospect of staying, which surprised me. I thought he might just be attracted to the idea of spending time with David, who is a good-looking young man. David seemed indifferent and just wanted to nurse his sore leg.

After a little more "Should I or shouldn't I?" by Dax, we were finally ready to leave. We each hugged or manfully shook hands with David. He apologized for holding us back, which he really hadn't because Karen's speed was not much faster than David crutching with his trekking poles. Once again we shouldered our packs, walked out of the lodge, and headed south down the trail through Phaplu.

Imposition

Just outside of Phaplu is the district government headquarters of Solu at Sallert. The main trail turned downhill toward the impressive compound of buildings. It would have been interesting to hike down to visit the government campus, but our trail narrowed and forked left uphill. We needed to make time and catch up to Purna and the kitchen crew.

As we put distance between Phaplu and us, the incline became steeper. Apparently well used by local traders and herdsmen, the trail's dirt was packed so hard that the trail had developed a U shape. This, along with the incline, made footing difficult.

Unfortunately, the rain that had drenched us during the last stage of our hike the night before had also soaked the narrow trail, making it very slippery.

Dax started muttering about not enjoying this. As the footing became more difficult, his muttering turned to whining. He slipped and fell to one knee. When he got up, he proclaimed in a shrieky tone of voice, "I'm not enjoying this! This is not working for me!" Then he announced he was not going any farther. He demanded that Sanga get his duffel and that he was going back to Phaplu and would stay at the lodge with David.

I started to argue with him to try to convince him not to quit the trek, but when he resisted, I got disgusted. I shook my head and said, "Fine, but I hope you realize what you're making Sanga do." Sanga quickly intervened and said not to worry, he would take care of it. Luckily, our porters were just behind us. Sanga stopped the porter carrying Dax's duffel and pulled it out of the doko. Sanga slung the duffel over his back and strapped his own large backpack in front so it rode on his chest instead of his back.

We were only about an hour out from the Number Lodge. Our farewells were brief and formal. Sanga began hiking back, with Dax following. I was pissed at Dax and headed up the trail, muttering to myself and shaking my head. Carl and Karen both looked a bit wide-eyed with surprise over these developments but didn't seem too upset by Dax's departure.

On one level, it made no sense to me. Dax was the most fit member of the group. Yes, he had trouble with the slipperiness of the trail and, despite his strength and fitness, his coordination is not particularly good. But I think the real problem was that he was not spiritually committed to experiencing Basa and so lacked the mental toughness to endure the discomfort of slipping and sliding on the trail to get there.

When we were in Ladakh in 1997, Dax endured altitude sickness, dehydration, and sunburn and did not want to quit when our leader, John Roskelley, ordered him to abandon the expedition due to his weakened condition. He was ready to fight Roskelley to continue but reluctantly acquiesced after Judy and I helped him see the sense of this decision. I don't know why he had not made the mental and emotional commitment to Basa. He was the only member of the group who had not contributed to the school project prior to the trek. But we only had to hike the rest of the day and then part of the next day and we would be there. Why surrender now?

Sanga would have to hike back to Phaplu, get Dax checked into the lodge, and then run down the trail as fast as he could to catch up to us. It was a great imposition for Dax to require Sanga to make this sacrifice of time and energy, but to Sanga it was just part of the job. He did not seem at all upset about the imposition, just disappointed that Dax was quitting.

I had no right to feel self-righteous about Dax requiring extra work of Sanga. One day during the 1996 Ladakh expedition, I thought I lost my camera. Halfway between our lunch stop and campsite for the night, I couldn't find it. After we arrived at camp, while we were getting ready for dinner, I told our group that I must have left my camera at the settlement where we had eaten lunch. Well, there was no way I could hike back to retrieve the camera that night. Our sirdar, Tsering Sherpa, said he would hike back and look for it. I told him he need not, but he did. We had hiked four hours after the lunch stop. He made the round trip on his own twice as fast as we had hiked, but that still required him to hike another four hours after a full day of hiking. When Tsering arrived back in camp long after the rest of us had finished eating dinner, he told me he had talked with locals who had watched us eating and they remembered seeing me take photos and put the camera back in my pack. It was a mystery. I had carefully searched my pack for the camera—I thought.

A day later, I discovered the camera in the bottom of my pack, hidden under a book. I don't know how or why I had not found it before then. I was so ashamed that Tsering had wasted all that time and energy in search of my camera that I did not tell him I found it. My guilt meant a larger tip for him, but I still bear the shame. So I had no right to feel too uppity about Sanga's extra effort for Dax.

Prayer Wheel

Now we followed Arjun. The trail became even more difficult, like a slippery roller coaster. Another hour onward, it finally flattened and the hiking became much easier. We passed a farmer carrying a bundle of hay in the typical Himalayan way. All we could see of him was his legs. To an American child, the farmer would look like a hay monster.

Around a bend, we discovered a little one-room temple just off the trail. It had a padlock on it, but because Carl and Karen were curious to see the inside of the temple, Arjun put down his pack and ran up a side trail leading to a couple of houses. He came back with a woman who told him the caretaker was working in a field, but she unlocked the door for us. Inside, bare wood walls surrounded one large prayer wheel. With the woman's permission, we turned the wheel. It was a release. Karen and Carl turned the wheel faster and began whooping with joy while they sprinted around the prayer wheel. They had the spirit.

It struck me once again how tolerant Tibetan Buddhism is. Imagine two strangers entering a church or mosque and whooping with joy. I know how my minister reacted when I was thirteen and he walked into the sanctuary and found two girls and

Karen and Carl turning a prayer wheel

me rolling around on the floor tickling each other and laughing. In New Delhi, a caretaker wielding a broom chased me from a mosque because out of curiosity I had walked in to look around and had forgotten I was supposed to take my shoes off before entering. And "unclean" sahibs are not even allowed inside many Hindu temples. Yet here we were, Karen and Carl whooping with joy and turning the prayer wheel while the local woman and Arjun watched with broad smiles on their faces.

Arjun, Karen, Carl, and I left the temple after warmly thanking our new friend for unlocking it for us. We each gave her a small offering to help maintain the temple. We walked off with a new lightness in our tread. Arjun was carrying Karen's pack, as he had since the first day on the trail, in front with his pack on the back, so he looked like a pregnant young man with a hump back. I patted his protuberant "belly" and asked if it was a boy or a girl. He didn't understand the joke at first, but after Karen explained it, Arjun laughed like it was the funniest joke he had ever heard. He knew we were happy, so he was happy.

We hiked and bantered in good humor until we saw Rudra standing at the top of a side trail waving and calling to us. We hiked up a ten-foot rise into a grassy kharka. Purna and his crew were already cooking lunch in the open field. They had spread out a tarp for us to relax on. So we plopped down and gratefully accepted cups of chilled Tang, bowls of peaches, and chapatti (thin, crisp, unleavened bread). It was pleasant to enjoy the view looking back at the country we had just hiked across.

Just after we started eating our lunch of cooked sardines, veggies, and ham sandwiches, Sanga came huffing up, dropped his pack, stretched his arms, and looked at us quizzically. He could tell something had changed in our mood since he had hiked off with Dax. We were joyful.

Karen, Carl, the whole crew, all of us felt a liberation and joy that had been lacking in our experience on this trek. But we had come alive and were infused with the richness of living in the moment and the joy of sharing the experience of being in this place.

16

DOWN TO THREE

Now we were only three—Carl, Karen, and me. Actually, we were twenty-three. Our crew consisted of twenty guys—sirdar Sanga, cook Purna, assistant sirdar Arjun, four kitchen boys (Pancha, Nirman, Kumar, and Rudra), and thirteen porters—a ridiculously large staff for three clients. Niru had staffed the trek for ten people. His devotion to the families of Basa would not allow him to "lay off" someone from a crew after a position on an expedition was offered. Subsistence farmers from villages in the Himalayas covet jobs on expeditions. To lose a job on an expedition would be a significant financial loss for the whole family. So even when he knew our group was only six instead of the expected ten, Niru kept all the guys on the crew who had originally been offered the job to staff the trek.

Niru staffed my previous groups with more personnel than other expedition companies I've used and companies with which I'm familiar. Ordinarily, one porter per client is a sufficient number of porters because carrying one duffel and a tent is a light load for a porter. A normal load would be two duffels and a tent. But there is also the kitchen equipment, meal tent, kitchen tent, toilet tent, and all the miscellaneous items, such as utensils, meal table, and the food, all of which must be carried by porters or kitchen boys. If it's a climbing expedition, then all the climbing gear and ropes are added to the porters' burdens. With only six clients in the beginning and three at the end, carrying for out trek was almost a vacation for the porters.

The kitchen boys carry everything the cook needs to set up the kitchen, but they travel light compared to the porters. The cook wants his kitchen staff to get to camp ahead of the trekkers to prepare dinner as early as possible. So the kitchen boys carry lighter loads than the porters, although much bigger loads than trekkers. The kitchen staff is normally the first to arrive at the campsite. Tents can be set up during or even after dinner, and the clients shouldn't need to get into their duffels until after dinner. Food and drink is the first priority after hiking all day.

The Crew

I try to make a point of learning all the names of crew members for groups I lead. For the Basa trek, I am ashamed to admit, I did not commit all the staff members' names to memory. And I didn't even take a picture of the assembled staff, as clients typically do.

I excused myself to some extent because we were pushing so hard and the trek was so short in the number of days on the trail with the crew. But it has bothered me since my first expedition that some clients on expeditions don't even learn the name of the porter carrying their gear. Some writers, including ones who have written for major publications, when describing the personnel in a mountaineering expedition, refer to the porters as an undifferentiated mass and call all of them Sherpas, even though there might not be a single Sherpa serving as a porter. Although the job of a porter is similar to that of a pack animal, each porter is a fellow human. Each is worthy of respect and deserves to be identified as an individual. Yet throughout this book, I have referred to them as "the porters" or "our porters." My apologies; they deserve better. As provided by Niru, our porters were:

1. Bhaktu Rai
2. Purna Bahadur Rai
3. Shankabir Rai
4. Mati Dhan Rai
5. Manke Rai
6. Dille Bhujel
7. Dhruba Nepali
8. Chandra Bahadur Bika
9. Harka Bika
10. Padam Bahadur Bhujel
11. Shankar Nepali
12. Bhim Bahadur Bika
13. Sabin Bhujel
14. Some Rai (Bill's porter/guide)

Together

After lunch, we had a fairly easy hike, with gradually increasing altitude. We passed through a couple of settlements. Sanga pointed out that the people we met at these settlements were not Sherpas. We met a Chetri family hiking home after celebrating Dasain with relatives in Phaplu. But most of the people we met along the trail east of Phaplu were Rai.

The trail continued to gain altitude. By late afternoon, Carl's altimeter read 11,000 feet. We topped out on the Phurlung Pass over Ratnagi Danda, a long mountain ridge overlooking a huge plunging valley. Somewhere below us on the other side of the river valley and around a few more hills was Basa. We couldn't see it yet, but the eager smiles on the faces of our crew members told us that their home village was not far.

They would have to wait another day. The sun was going down and the long descent on the other side of Ratnagi Danda would take too long to handle that day. Sanga, Purna, and Arjun had decided we would camp high on the ridge at a place they called Kanku. There is no such place marked on my "Himalayan Map House" trail map or in my Lonely Planet guidebook. But I trusted Sanga's judgment and the best news was that we would be in Basa before lunchtime the next day.

Last campsite before Basa

This would be our last night of camping on the trail because tomorrow we'd be in Basa and the night after that we had to be back in Phaplu to catch our scheduled flight for Katmandu the following day. It would be the last day our entire crew would be together. We would only need a few porters to carry our duffels back to Phaplu. The company gear would stay in Basa for the time being, as would most of the guys in our crew.

The view from our campsite was breathtakingly beautiful. We looked out over the great valley we would be crossing in the morning and then crossing back the next day. We were tired. It had been another long day of hiking and arriving in camp after dusk. But the crew was not tired and there was a party atmosphere among the guys. We didn't have a last-night party, as is customary the last night of an expedition, because it wasn't the last night of the trek. In fact, the hardest day was two days in the future. It was unusual, however, to spend the last night before parting with crew members without some kind of celebration.

At least, Purna outdid himself. We enjoyed a seven-course feast, including Sherpa stew with beef, rice, potatoes, and veggies; chicken strips; fresh salad; canned fruit; and tapioca and rice puddings.

Carl, Karen, Sanga, Arjun, and I sat in the meal tent talking for a time after we finished eating. Usually, the sirdar would leave clients alone to socialize in the meal tent after the table was cleared. He might help the cook clean up the kitchen or make sure the porters had eaten and found places to sleep. If the porters planned to sleep in the meal tent, the sirdar would gently encourage the clients not to linger too long so the porters could move in and crash. But that night up on the Ratnagi Danda, the five of us lingered. There was a lot of room in the meal tent around the table with only the five of us.

Arjun and Karen had become close friends, having spent many hours walking the trail together. Since Arjun was carrying

Karen's pack, they had been stuck together whether they liked it or not. They liked it, and had not tired of each other's company.

Carl had become very popular with the whole crew. His mellow disposition and large size was endearing to the much smaller Nepalese men. His size 17 hiking boots and great height had earned him the nickname "Yeti" with the guys. It was sweet to see him joking around with them. At first they smiled shyly, but when Sanga let the guys know that Carl thought the nickname amusing, they were given license to joke openly with Carl. Kumar, or one of the other kitchen boys, would point at Carl, pretend to look wide-eyed with fear, and whisper, "Yeti!" Carl would let out a roar and then the whole crew would laugh hysterically. The joke was replayed at least a couple of times each day, but no one tired of it.

The five of us realized this trek was becoming something very special. Carl and Karen should not have been the two to have made it this far. Carl was fifty-nine years old with lots of hiking and camping experience, but this was his first trek. He had been involved in protracted custody litigation for months before departing for Nepal. Consequently, he had not trained for the trek nearly as much as he had planned. Of course, he had expected an easy introductory cultural trek and not "Survivor Nepal."

Carl told us that night that so much of his mental, emotional, and spiritual energy was spent in the litigation and related family matters, he just didn't have any energy to hike or work out in the last few months leading up to the trek. Getting away from it all to come to Nepal was a relief. Carl said that, instead of being run down by hiking the trail to Basa, he was reenergized. He felt himself being freed from the psychic weight the custody litigation had put on him and, as he let go of that burden, he became lighter and stronger.

Karen had opened her own psychotherapy practice just a month before her flight to Katmandu. Rather than a joyous occasion, it followed a year of struggles with her former partner. She had been so preoccupied with resolving the partnership issues and then setting up her own office, that she was too drained to condition for the trek or even break in her hiking boots.

Arjun's English was at about the level of a five-year old, so I'm not sure how much of the discussion he understood. He nodded a lot and had an understanding and concerned look on his face while we talked.

Sanga has a very curious mind. Earlier in the trek, he had told me all things about people from the West, especially Americans, fascinate him. Sanga listened closely to Carl's and Karen's descriptions of the challenges they faced back home in their professional and personal lives. I could see by his earnest expression he was trying to integrate into his understanding of life in America the information gained from listening to Karen and Carl. He was trying to imagine having these concerns and living in their world.

Regardless of the great cultural differences between us, there was a bond of understanding and an easy and open willingness to share a piece of our lives sitting together in that tent up on the mountain ridge called Ratnagi Danda. Tomorrow we would see what awaited us in Basa. Karen, Carl, and I would be the third group of white people to visit the village in its collective memory.

As we parted for the night—Karen, Carl, and I to sleep in our separate tents and Sanga and Arjun to join the crew in the outbuilding serving as kitchen—we heard the porters laughing and singing in the kitchen. They were having their own celebration. They would be home in the morning.

17

BASA

I was eager to get out of camp and begin the last stage of the hike to Basa. So was everyone in our group, members and staff alike. The weariness in our limbs from the ten- and twelve-hour hikes the last four days was forgotten in anticipation of reaching our goal before noon. While Karen, Carl, and I were organizing our duffels and kits, Arjun and the porters tore down the meal tent. The sky was clear as the sun came up. Arjun knew it would be pleasant to eat breakfast outside instead of in the meal tent. He instructed the kitchen boys to set the breakfast table on open ground, so we could enjoy the view from the steep eastern slope of the Ratnagi Danda, overlooking the vast valley we would hike through to Basa.

The slope was latticed with switchbacks. According to my trail map, it is over 5,200 feet from the top of the pass down to the bridge across the Kaku Khola in the gut of the valley. Because the eastern slope of the Ratnagi Danda is so steep, the trail switches back and forth in the early stage of the hike below the top of the ridge and then traverses around the side of the mountain, so that the actual hiking distance to the bridge must be five to ten times greater than the straight-line distance. Purna gave us each a sack lunch and then we took off hiking as quickly as we could down the steep winding trail toward the river below.

It became increasingly hot as the sun's ascent matched our descent. Halfway down to the river, I stripped down to hiking shorts, using my shirt as a sweat towel. Even the porters stripped off their long-sleeved shirts to reduce their body heat in the hot sun.

We didn't hike through any villages on the descent, but we did walk by several terraced farm settlements, each inhabited by Rai people. The eastern slope of the Ratnagi Danda is a great green giant, covered by lush flora and pretty little terraced farms of wheat and barley. Despite the heat, Sanga and Arjun were in high spirits leading us down to the bridge across the Kaku Khola. We were in Rai country and the guys were close to home.

The bridge across the Kaku Khola is a marvel. It is one of the longest bridges I have crossed in the Himalayas. The bridge is solidly built with steel cables and a steel-planked base. It vibrated

Crossing the Kaku Khola suspension bridge

with each step and swayed in the wind. It was fun and a bit of an adrenaline rush to walk across it.

Our whole crew of porters, Sanga, Arjun, Karen, Carl, and I hiked together down the flank of the Ratnagi Danda and across the bridge. After we were across the bridge, I didn't want to hold back any longer. I let Sanga know I would be hiking out ahead of everyone and picked up my pace. Although Basa is not designated on my trail map, Niru had marked on the map where to cut off the main trail, so I felt confident I would be able to find the village. I hurried through a large village called Losku. My map indicated it has a temple just off the trail, but I didn't stop to check it out. I wanted to get to Basa.

After another hour of solo hiking, I came to another and even larger village called Sombare. I later learned Sombare is where the Himalayan Secondary School is that Ganesh and Sanga graduated from.

The trail split in Sombare and there was a little market on one leg of the trail. I was tempted to stop and enjoy browsing through the market, but my desire to get to Basa was stronger so I didn't tarry. I double-timed through the village, but the trail split again and I became insecure about whether I was still on the correct trail or not. An elderly man wearing a topi was taking his constitutional, so I asked him in my pidgin Nepali if I was on the trail to Basa, "Yo Basa jaane baato ho?" (Is this the trail to Basa?) I couldn't understand his reply, but he waved me on the way I was going, so I stayed on the trail right up to a charpi (outhouse) where the trail ended. When I passed him on my way back to find the correct trail, he smiled in a friendly way and walked with me, chattering away in a language I did not understand at all. Apparently, he had not meant to trick me and had not misdirected me out of malice. He must have interpreted my question about the trail to Basa as request for the location of the nearest toilet. I guessed that the old gent only spoke the local Rai language.

When we parted, I hustled on down the trail. After another hour, I discovered a group of eight men wearing topis, gathered at a trail junction. At first I didn't know what to make of them. They were holding little drums and wooden flutes. They waved at me like they wanted me to stop and talk to them, but then they became rather shy and didn't seem to know what to do. None of them spoke English, and I had lost confidence in my limited Nepali. So I just repeatedly asked, "Basa?"

Heads moved in various directions in response to my question. Nepalis tend to move their heads in a circular motion to indicate the affirmative, and to look away to indicate the negative. So I interpreted the head waggling response as "Yes, this is the way to Basa." Then it dawned on me that these men were the greeting party from the village. That was why they were holding musical instruments.

I wanted to hike down to the village, but with the utmost politeness the eldest member of the musical group restrained me. I inferred that they wanted me to await the arrival of the rest of our group, so that they could lead us into the village.

The men indicated I should sit down and relax. I know the Nepali word meaning stay or rest, *basne*. So I used the word, emphasizing the last syllable with a higher tone or lilt in my voice, which is the way a question is asked in Nepali. I didn't understand any of the words the men said in response, but I did understand that they agreed I should rest when one of the guys with a drum gestured toward the stone wall next to us and patted a spot on it as a place for me to sit down. So I sat on the wall, took several granola bars out of my pack, and offered to share. The men chuckled but did not hold out their hands to take the snack. They seemed amused and pleased, but only the youngest fellow let me put one of the granola bars in his hand. The guys continued to smile shyly at me. I sensed a calmness and friendliness as well as curiosity in the way they watched me eat the granola bar. I scrounged the book I was reading out of my backpack and read and snacked and waited.

About twenty minutes later, Sanga, Carl, Arjun, and Karen came huffing down the trail. As soon as the group of men from Basa saw the others, they jumped up excitedly. They looked delighted as they briefly conferred with Sanga and Arjun in their local language. Sanga nodded vigorously several times, and then the men lifted their instruments. With great dignity, they began thumping on the drums and tooting on the flute-like instruments. Sanga gestured for us to follow and down the trail we walked in single file.

Welcome

The narrow trail descended about nine-hundred feet with one long switchback and then the village appeared below us. It was astonishing to see that one hundred or more people had gathered and were lined up in an area between two stone buildings with blue tin roofs. The buildings were tucked into the side of the steep hill we were descending. I thought I recognized the building to the left as the schoolhouse from photos Niru had sent me.

The trail leveled off on a narrow shoulder and then we were at the entrance to the village. There was a hand-painted "Welcome" sign atop wood poles ringed with flowers. As we walked under the sign, the band members, Sanga, and Arjun peeled off. A long line of women and children met us. Every person in line had a flower garland similar to a Hawaiian lei. As Karen, Carl, and I walked down the line, the women and children placed leis over our heads. After the garland dropped around one of our necks, the person who bestowed it smiled shyly or excitedly while

First contact; Basa musicians above the village

giving the traditional Nepali greeting of "namaste" with bowed head and palms placed together.

The leis piled up so high around our necks and over our faces that we had to take some off so we could see. Apparently, every family in the village and surrounding area had turned out to welcome us and had made flower garlands to give us as tokens of greeting.

Poor Carl. He has allergies. He did his best to control his sinuses, but his face was turning red, his eyes were watering, and he was beginning to sneeze. But what was he to do? He is such a good sport and kind soul; he tried his best not to show any discomfort to avoid putting a damper on the villagers' enthusiastic welcome.

At the end of the line of women and children, we were guided to a line of men. As we passed along that line, each man gave the

Flowery welcome: (right to left) Carl, Karen, and me with flower garlands

namaste greeting or shook our hands. Some greeted us in both the Nepali and English style. A few of the men took my hand and touched their forehead with my fore knuckle and then kissed my hand. Several placed katas (silk scarves) around our necks over the flower garlands.

Sanga was standing in the middle of the grounds. He indicated we should sit in chairs set up behind a table in front of a rock wall by the hillside. The villagers settled onto benches set up around the grounds, squatted on their haunches, or leaned against the walls of the two buildings. After we were seated, Sanga made a brief statement in the local language to the gathered crowd and then sat down in the chair to my right.

A group of men, who appeared to be the village elders, sat on a bench across from us. One of them stood up and began making a speech. Sanga whispered that he was the chairman of the school committee. Sanga didn't bother to translate for us most of the chairman's speech, which lasted about twenty minutes, but just explained he was speaking the local Rai language and was welcoming us and talking about the school. The school building, Sanga told us, was the building behind the elders, as I had guessed.

The speech might have gotten boring for Karen, Carl, and me except that, while the chairman was talking, village women lined up to pour cups of their homemade rakshi (distilled spirits) for us. Apparently, almost every woman in the village brought a pitcher of her best rakshi to the ceremony and expected each of us to drink a cup. At first it was wonderful, because well-made rakshi is tasty, and we were served many different flavors, among them rice, millet, and plum. But it can also be quite potent, and we had hiked several hours under a hot sun and only eaten a sack lunch since breakfast.

After downing a couple of cups, I resorted to taking only one sip from the rest of the pitchers offered but exuberantly thanked each pitcher bearer. I whispered to Karen and Carl to follow my lead and just take sips or we'd get so drunk, we'd fall out of our chairs. Karen had already adopted my strategy, but Carl had trouble turning down any gift and was about three sheets to the wind by the time the chairman's speech was over.

Next, the chairman of the Committee of Supervisors for the local government gave a speech. The rakshi kept coming and Sanga again didn't bother to translate the speech. He just explained that Basa was one of several villages in the area served by this elected committee for development of the villages within their jurisdiction. The chairman was thanking us on behalf of each of the different settlements and villages within the district.

After the second speech ended, Sanga told me he was going to introduce me and I would need to give a speech to the village, which he would translate. In his introduction, Sanga told the villagers the details of the fundraising campaign for the school and that we had already raised $1,400, which had been delivered to Niru in Katmandu.

Sanga had not forewarned me of the expectation of a speech, but being an experienced trial lawyer, flapping my jaw is what I'm paid to do, so I wasn't nervous, especially being fortified by multiple cups of rakshi. I figured one way I could score points with the villagers was to keep it short and sweet. So I thanked them for their wonderful welcome and told them that our friends from the United States and South Africa who could not come with us sent their greetings too. I said it was an honor and a privilege to be able to help finish the school. I related how I had become friends with Niru, Ganesh, Sanga, Arjun, and many other men from the village who had served my trekking groups so well, and thanked the village and all its families for producing such fine people.

When I finished speaking, there was no applause or cheers, which was momentarily disconcerting, but then I remembered there had been no clapping or cheering for the other speakers. Nevertheless, I think the speech was well received, because each person who caught my eye smiled and bowed.

The form of expression of appreciation by the villagers reflected a delightful gentleness of character. No loud or violent clapping or cheering, just smiling and bowing the head with hands held together to express respect. It was a lovely experience to have been granted the privilege to speak to the whole village on behalf of my thirty-some friends who had donated or pledged to the Basa School Project.

Sanga then pulled a notebook and cash purse out of his pack. He made an announcement that I did not understand, as he was speaking the local dialect, and then began calling out names. After he called a name, either a student or parent would approach, Sanga would give the person a certain amount of rupees, record it in the notebook, and have the recipient countersign the record of payment.

Sanga explained that the French NGO, Sol Himal, provided stipends to the families of students who graduated from the Basa school and then went on to the school in Sombare. I didn't understand why, but after each person received the payment, they thanked Karen, Carl, and me by kissing our hands or bowing to us. I asked Sanga if the villagers understood that the stipends were not from us, and he assured me that the villagers knew the French group paid the stipends. They just wanted to express their thanks to us for being associated with helping the school. I wondered if in the minds of the villagers all "white people" were related in some way.

I loved the welcoming ceremony, and Carl, Karen, and I agreed it was probably the closest we would ever come to being treated like celebrities. But I was also anxious to inspect the school and meet the teachers. Sanga informed me, however, that the teachers were too ashamed of the quality of their English to meet with us. His wife is the head teacher, so if anyone would have been able to persuade them, it should have been Sanga. But he explained that the three women were just too shy, and he would show me the school building.

Basa School

I was disappointed because I wanted to show the teachers the sample workbooks I had brought with me to make sure they would be appropriate for the school. A friend with the Indiana Department of Education had arranged to donate educational materials sufficient to supply all of the students with workbooks and supplies for math, social studies, and English. But Sanga said he would go over the materials with me and then explain to the teachers what would be shipped to the school. He assured me the teachers would be thrilled with whatever we could provide. After I saw the classrooms, I understood.

The only teaching materials were chalkboards with no erasers and handmade posters; no books or tablets. There were a few rough benches for students to sit on; no desks or chairs. It pulled at my heartstrings to see such beautiful and eager children and to imagine what their classes must be like without any teaching materials or supplies other than the enthusiasm of their teachers and rudimentary posters hung by string on the patched walls of the little classroom.

The floor of the building had a three-inch crack running the width of the building wall to wall. The walls were bare plaster and the wood frames of the windows were rotting. Niru was right to request that the funds already raised be immediately al-

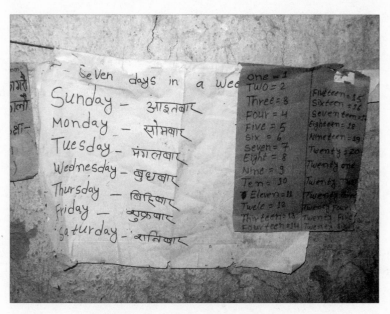

Basa School instructional aid poster

located to patch the floor, paint and seal the walls and window frames, and build more benches so all the students could at least sit on benches. I felt tremendously gratified to realize that, after the pledges were fulfilled, the area behind the school could be cleared to create a playground with a rock wall for security, since there is about a 500-foot drop-off at one end of the field where the playground was to be created. Best of all, we would have enough money to hire the two teachers needed to add fourth and fifth grade classes.

I discovered one more issue the project would have to resolve. The charpi outside the school building was so disgusting it was padlocked and couldn't be used. From a previous project for another village, I knew that for a few hundred dollars a compost toilet could be purchased. The entire village could use it or reserve it only for the schoolchildren. I added a compost toilet to my list.

For the moment, I knew exactly why the hell we were here in Nepal. To receive the love of this village and to give of our material wealth so these children would have better lives.

18

A DAY IN BASA

We spent the rest of the day visiting homes throughout the village and meeting the families of our crew members. We were followed everywhere by a gaggle of children who wanted to hold our hands and lead us to the next home. At each home, the matriarch of the house insisted we try her rakshi. Thankfully, we were also offered food, usually fried potatoes, yoghurt with fruit, and plates of dal bhat (rice with lentils).

The conversations were in the local Rai dialect with Sanga translating. Carl was almost sleepwalking from his intake of rakshi, but smiling happily and agreeing with everything anyone said. Karen and I were both feeling pretty tipsy from all of the rakshi, so my memory of our visits to homes around the village is a little hazy. But I was conscious of the warm glow of friendly hospitality from all of the families we visited. We were asked questions about life in our "villages," and we joked about guys from the village in our crew or who I knew from other expeditions. The conversations were light and friendly and expressed polite curiosity on both sides.

I asked a few political questions, but the only one that sparked any interest (and I think it was mainly Sanga's interest) was how the change of the national constitution would affect the village. Sanga told me that at the next election a mayor of the village would be chosen for the first time. The mayor would take over some of the duties of the Committee of Supervisors. I asked if Niru would run for mayor. Sanga replied with a laugh, "No, because Niru-ji does not want to live in village all the time."

One of Niru's sisters maintains his family home in Basa and he stays there when he visits the village, but his primary residence is now in Katmandu. I asked if Niru would try to influence the election of mayor. I could tell that this concept seemed strange to Sanga. To me, it was an obvious political issue. Niru is the only significant employer for the village, and his work with Sol Himal and my group had brought about the development of a village school and stipends for many students' families. Sanga had previously told me that, directly or indirectly, Niru helped to support two hundred people in the Basa area. So, in my mind, he must be considered the Godfather of Basa. Sanga acknowledged the great good Niru had done for the people of Basa, but assured me Niru would not try to influence the choice of mayor. And he said, "We know the men who will run for mayor. We know everyone and who would be good man."

Families in every home within walking distance of the school asked us to visit their houses, but Sanga reluctantly restricted our visits to five or six homes. (With all the rakshi I consumed, my focus wasn't sharp enough to remember whether it was five or six.) Whenever Sanga apologetically informed a family that we would be unable to visit a particular home, the matriarch of the family would urge us to accept another cup of rakshi or a slice of bread or other food offering. Of course we accepted every offering, so we were stuffed as well as drunk. Our visit had created a holiday atmosphere throughout the village, and most of the adults we encountered in walking from home to home were getting tight on their own rakshi.

Like the Sherpas, Rai are matriarchal. In the homes with grandmothers, the grandmother was in charge of initially welcom-

Sanga's mother, Durga Rai

ing us and offering food. After we settled on the floor, the grand-mother would get a conversation started, with Sanga translating, and would then instruct younger members of the family to make sure our cups stayed full and our plates were heaped with food.

It was a special pleasure to be welcomed into Sanga's home by his mother, Durga Rai, and to meet Ganesh's mom, Dilmaya Rai.

Most of the houses we visited were made of chiseled stones with blue tin roofs. Some had plaster walls with wood shingled roofs or straw roofs. The entryway doors were less than six feet high and Carl usually cracked his head on the lintel as he en-tered. The windows were open spaces, but could be closed off with swinging hinged wooden casements in bad weather. Most of the houses had one central room where all activities took place, including cooking over a fire pit, dining, and sleeping. The floors were hard-packed dirt.

Niru's house in Basa

Each of the homes we visited had a few sheep or cattle and terraced plots of wheat, hay, millet, barley, corn, or rice. Tall grass covers the uncultivated land between the houses. Paths through the grass fields connect one homestead to another. There are no commercial buildings and no marketplace. Each family grows and raises its own food. Each home also has a still for making rakshi.

The more prosperous homes we visited, like Sanga's and Ganesh's, displayed brass platters in the central room of the house. Sanga explained that, in addition to crops and animals, a family's wealth is determined by the jewelry the women wear and the ability to display decorative cookware. All of the village women we met wore ornaments in their noses. Some of the women had just a simple nose ring or stud, but many, especially the matriarchs, wore elaborate gold jewelry that looked like a small mobile hanging from their nose, called a bullaki, according to Sanga. The

A man and two children in Basa

more prosperous women also wore gold and silver bracelets. All of the women wore long necklaces. Some of the necklaces were beaded and others made from gold coins. Another interesting expression of prosperity and respect within the Rai community, which Niru had described to me, is a series of corn husks tied to a bamboo pole in front of the house. This thangra provides a history of the success of the family's crops.

The men of the village wore much less interesting clothes than the women. They wore no visible jewelry or adornments. Other than the topi hat, I saw no consistency or style unique to the village or to Rai culture expressed in the men's clothing. They wore a mixture of handmade clothing and manufactured jackets and t-shirts. Presumably, the jackets and t-shirts were given by client members of expeditions or were Chinese-made articles purchased at the Sombare market.

Each home we visited was a working farmstead. I found it interesting and charming that every home has a flower garden. These folks are subsistence farm families, yet they have a deep appreciation of beauty. To value aesthetics enough to devote a bit of their land to a flower garden reflects a character in the community that I find utterly delightful. No matter that they don't have access to most art forms available in the modern world, they create art through a form they know—planting and cultivating.

Every foot of cultivatable land in Basa is valuable since agriculture is sustenance, yet the villagers use this valuable resource to create beauty for the sake of beauty—flowers in Basa.

19

A NIGHT IN BASA

By the time we finished visiting homes around the village, dusk was settling on Basa. Sanga led Karen, Carl, and me back to the school grounds, where our crew had set up our three tents. Although most of the guys had melted away to their own homes during the festivities, they had managed to set up our tents and place our duffels inside the tents. Our crew had inflated and laid out Therm-a-rests, sleeping bag liners, and pillows in each tent. Hot water bottles were placed at the end of each Therm-a-rest.

Sanga told us a dance performance by current students and graduates of the Basa school was scheduled for our benefit that evening. The older students, he explained, now attended secondary school in Sombare. He was a little nervous about the performance because Sanga's wife, whose name is Nanda Kumari Rai, was the dance instructor and in charge of the performance. The kids had been practicing for weeks. Sanga told us that Nanda had also designed outfits for the performers. The students' families had sewn the outfits the performers would wear from Nanda's pattern.

Before the performance, we were allowed about an hour to nap and clean up in the privacy of our tents. The privacy was limited in that children hung around our tents the entire time.

Karen reading to Toulashea

They were extremely curious to see anything and everything we had in our duffels.

One nine-year old girl, named Toulashea, attached herself to Karen, holding her hand throughout the afternoon. Karen showed Toulashea her clothes and personal kit and then read to her from the workbooks I had brought for the school. Carl took photos of the kids and let them see their own images on his digital camera. I tried to nap and sleep off the rakshi, but gave up after fifteen minutes and let the kids see what was inside my tent.

Just after dark, the entire village assembled again on the school grounds. The students sat in a group against the stone wall at the end of the grounds. I was surprised to see Nanda set up a battery-powered boom box on the table used by the village elders during the welcoming ceremonies. After Nanda's brief description of the

Kids looking in my tent

program, the kids began to dance, accompanied by instrumental folk music of drums and woodwinds on a cassette recording on the boom box.

The girls wore brightly colored wrap skirts and multicolored checked blouses. The boys wore smart-looking pajama-style outfits with embroidered vests and brightly patterned topi hats. Most of the dances were coed, though a few were performed only by the boys and a few only by the girls. To the more dramatic dances with thumping drum beats from the boom box, the audience clapped along with the beat. Sanga explained that the dances told stories through the movements, and all the villagers knew the stories. (Like the leis used to welcome visitors, this was another interesting parallel with Pacific culture: storytelling through dance.)

Dancing students

The younger kids looked very serious and were careful to follow the older students and to make each step and movement correctly. The older kids moved very gracefully and danced with gusto and broad smiles on their faces. They strutted and swooned, their lithe limbs moving in perfect timing with the rhythm of the music. They were having a great time. Karen, Carl, and I jumped to our feet and clapped and shouted "Bravo!" after the last set.

Our day in Basa was finally coming to a close. After receiving bows from each of the dancers, the three of us went over to Nanda and thanked her enthusiastically. She was so shy, but pride in her students beamed out of her lovely round face. She smiled demurely and thanked us for enjoying the program.

Under the Stars

Several kids hung around Karen, Carl, and me after the program was over and villagers had headed home. The children didn't want to leave us, but parents chided them and, I'm sure, told their children we needed to get our sleep just as the kids needed their sleep. Sanga asked if we were ready to go to bed and whether we needed anything. We told him to go home and enjoy the company of his wife and little son, Saugat Rai. We could tell Sanga was very happy about the success of the program Nanda had devised for us. We kidded him about getting to spend the night with his wife, reminding him he was still on the job. He promised to perform especially well.

Kidding aside, it was a great treat for Sanga, Arjun, and all the guys to get to spend a night with their families while working a trek. The whole village was happy. I did not want to let go of that warm glow. But like the curmudgeon who is unhappy until he finds the thorns among the roses, there were troubling thoughts itching at the back of my mind behind the suffused happiness of such a special day.

Carl, Karen, and I were physically exhausted, but we weren't ready to shut down for the night. We stood outside our tents and listened to the subtle noises of the village turning in for the night. We looked up at the huge starry sky. There was no light pollution, since there is no electricity and no artificial illumination in Basa, aside from our headlamps. It may be trite to say, but the stars were so bright they looked close enough to touch. What a day.

Basa seemed Edenic. Although it lacks any modern amenities, even a water system, the villagers seemed to have such a wonderful appreciation of beauty; from our welcome with the flower garlands to the aesthetics of the design of the houses and the grace of the children's dancing, an appreciation of beauty was threaded into our experience of Basa. Perhaps the religion of the

Rai people contributes to the appreciation of beauty in Basa. As noted previously, Rai are animists. While they believe in one over-arching God, they also believe that all things and creatures have spirits. So all things, animate or inanimate, deserve some degree of respect or deference, because every thing has its own spirit.

Another quality of the community that impressed me was the ease with which its members interacted regardless of social standing. Yet Ganesh and Niru had warned me before we planned the trek that the caste system is practiced in Basa. The way it is practiced, from what I was told, sounded relatively benign compared to orthodox Hinduism. Niru and Ganesh explained that low caste people are not allowed to enter the homes of higher castes. The vast majority of people in the Basa area are Rai, but there are also Chettri, Damai, and Kami. Niru sent me the caste demographics of Basa 6, the official name of the village. The total population is 357, and of that number, 282 are Rai, 56 are Damai, 13 are Kami, and 6 are Chettri.

Rai and Chettri are the high castes; Damai and Kami are the lower castes. Talking to Ganesh on previous treks about his life in the village, he described incidents of having low caste friends in his house and the friends having to run out the back door when Ganesh's parents came home. Niru explained that if a lower caste person is visiting a higher caste member, the lower caste person may only be served food outside the house in accordance with the caste tradition.

Niru and Ganesh claimed that the higher caste members in Basa do not treat lower caste members badly and younger members of the community do not believe the system is fair and would prefer not to follow it. The tradition hangs on, however, because the older people insist on maintaining it. Niru told me the Damai sew clothes and play traditional musical instruments at marriage ceremonies, and the Kami make metal tools. These are respected and useful trades.

I asked Niru how it came about that people other than Rai live in Basa, since the Rai had originally settled in the valleys all around this part of Solu. He explained that a Chettri came as a teacher to instruct locals in Nepali, when several decades ago the government first made an effort to teach the entire population of Nepal the national language. According to Niru, in ancient times, the Rai had one language, and the ancient Rai language was even a written language with sacred texts. But the ancient language and all the written texts were lost long ago. So each valley developed its own dialect of the Rai language. The local people were happy to welcome a teacher of a new language into their community. The Chettri teacher of Nepali stayed in Basa and his family joined him. Over time, Damai and Kami came to the area to offer their skills as tradesmen to the local people. Some stayed and acquired their own land, and some eventually married into Rai families, so there are several "mixed" families within the community, I learned from Niru.

Niru also told me that I would be able to identify the lower caste people from the higher ones in Basa, because the lower caste people are poorer and have smaller plots of land. There was a notable difference in the size and quality of materials used in the homes, in that the larger ones were made of chiseled stone with aluminum roofs and the poorer ones used more wood in the construction and had thatched roofs. I noticed little difference in terms of the quality of the clothing worn by villagers, but differences in the amount and quality of jewelry worn by women was noticeable. And the wealthier families displayed a few decorative items, such as brass and gold platters and plates on the interior walls of their homes. But as much as the caste system is ingrained in the traditions of Basa, I could not tell whether a person was higher or lower caste by observing behavior and interactions among the villagers. There was no detectable discrimination in the way people behaved toward each other. All kids in the village attend the school and are treated the same by the teachers, regardless of caste, Sanga assured me.

The caste system is inherently offensive to me, but I did not witness any oppression due to the tradition. It is an essentially oppressive system because limitations are placed on people as a result of the fortune or misfortune of birth. But the caste system does contribute to social stability, as long as the community accepts it as the norm. The terrible anxieties about choosing the right career and then devoting decades of life to climbing the socioeconomic ladder, so common in our culture, do not occur in a village culture in which socioeconomic position is largely determined by birth through a caste system. In that sense, I can understand that the caste system is an aspect of the communal equilibrium of Basa.

Another quality of the village people of Basa I pondered that night before falling asleep was their emotional honesty. I had not encountered a community of people in my travels around the world that seemed so comfortable expressing emotion. The villagers expressed delight at meeting us. They expressed extreme gratitude for us raising money for the school, to the point of tears and kissing my hand and cheek. Even shyness was not hidden in the sense of trying to cover it with fake confidence. And we would discover when we left the next day, the open expression of sadness, with tears and pulling on our shirtsleeves by people of all ages not wanting us to leave.

But there was one feature of life in Basa that contrasted to a paradise in my mind: alcoholism. That was a thorn among the roses. Every home we visited had a still. By the end of the day, several people we encountered were clearly drunk from their own rakshi. We were drunk too, but there is a difference between the happy drunk of a festive occasion and a routine drunk. What caused a twitching in the back of my mind was that several peo-

Welcome sign and campsite in Basa

ple in the village had the appearance of being regular drunks, not the occasional happy drunk.

Sanga told me that every family had its own still and that rakshi was always available in all the homes, but during our visit he did not mention alcoholism as a problem for the village. Lack of education for the children was Sanga's chief concern. In my correspondence with Niru after returning to the States and reflecting back on my experience in Basa, I raised the subject. Niru confirmed that alcoholism is a real problem for the village, and he related that it creates problems for some families when a mother or father turns to drink and neglects farming duties.

Pushing that little irritant to the back of my own rakshi-induced euphoria that magical night in Basa, it seemed to me the community is like a delicate flower, perfectly balanced in proportion. Unable to sleep, I worried again about how tourism would affect the communal equilibrium, the flower of Basa. The same questions went round in my mind. Was Niru right to start the process toward modernization of Basa? Was I doing the right thing to help move the process forward? Where would it all lead? Would the flower wither and die? For me, that was the big hidden thorn in the roses. But I had to get to sleep. I pushed the worry out of my mind and fell asleep, wondering what delights the morning in Basa would bring.

20

LEAVING BASA

The crowing of roosters awakened me. Before I was out of my sleeping bag, little friends with gimlet eyes and devilish grins were outside my tent. They peered through the tent fly and chattered and giggled while I organized my kit and duffel for the day's hike. I zippered the tent flap to dress in private. As soon as I emerged, several kids grabbed my hands to walk with me across the grounds to the school building where Purna was preparing breakfast for Karen, Carl, and me.

Villagers began to assemble on the grounds outside the school while Purna cooked. The village children were fascinated by everything about the three American visitors. They were curious to see us eat. Nepalese villagers use the fingers of their right hands for eating; they don't use utensils. So I think the children wanted to watch Carl, Karen, and me eat breakfast using knives, forks, and spoons. But to give us some privacy, our mother hen, Sanga, shooed the kids out of the classroom when we began eating. Only Karen's little favorite, Toulashea, was allowed to stay by her side.

By the time we finished eating and packing our duffels, the village elders were seated at the table outside the school. Chairs and a table were again set up for us on the other side of the grounds. Villagers stood, moved school benches to sit on, or squatted around the grounds. Sanga had not warned us, but it was apparent that a departure ceremony was to be held for us. We again took the seats of honor across from the village elders.

Three members of the Committee of Supervisors gave speeches. Sanga was too busy to translate as he was bustling around making sure our porters packed the duffels, tents, and all the kitchen gear, which needed to be carried back to Phaplu. Arjun's English was not sufficient to translate most of the speeches, but he tried. He told us we were being thanked again for helping with the school and visiting the village. The speeches were not as lengthy as they had been the afternoon before. Perhaps Sanga had informed the committee members that we had to hike to Phaplu, and so not as much time should be given to the departure ceremony as the welcome. We really did need to start our hike as soon as possible.

Last cup of rakshi in Basa

Bringing Progress to Paradise

After each speech, the elders stood, smiled at us, and bowed in unison in our direction with palms together. It was not quite the Temptations, but it was a lovely gesture that the village elders had taken the time to plan out their speeches and to bow to us in unison.

The grandmothers lined up again to offer us cups of rakshi, but Sanga, at my request, explained that we shouldn't drink before a long day's hike. I was not asked to speak, which was just as well, because I was beginning to worry about our ability to make the hike back to Phaplu. When the speeches were finished, Karen, Carl, and I stood together and executed bows with the namaste hand position, first toward the table of elders, and then in all directions around the grounds while trying to make eye contact with as many of the gathered villagers as possible.

Karen receiving flower garlands

Matriarchs of the village: three Rai women

We needed to get going up the trail to Phaplu, but it was difficult to leave. Children tugged at our elbows and shirtsleeves and wanted us to play with them and take pictures of them. Sanga sent the porters ahead. But our departure was delayed, because Nanda organized the women and children into a receiving line with leis and katas to hang around our necks before we could leave the village. The village band thumped and tootled while we made our way down the line and again received colorful garlands and filmy katas from at least one member of each of the families of the village.

Before we reached the end of the receiving line, the three schoolteachers stopped Karen, Carl, and me to pin on our shirts brooches of little figures made of colored straw. I was given three extras for the three members of our group who did not make it to Basa. Sanga's wife, Nanda, said to me in perfect English, belying

Leaving Basa; the whole village accompanied us

her insecurity about the quality of her English, "Thank you very much for helping our children and coming to our village." Then she kissed my cheek.

By the time we reached the end of the line, once again so many leis were strung around our necks we had to remove some of the garlands to see the trail in front of us. Before we were allowed to begin the hike up the steep trail out of the village, the old women kissed our cheeks and old men and children wept openly as we slung our packs and readied ourselves for the hike to Phaplu. Several of the men, who I think were of the lower castes, touched my hand to their foreheads and then kissed my hand and cheeks. They had tears in their eyes. Three leathered old matriarchs, led by Sanga's mother, Durga, stopped us a last time and kissed our cheeks and tried to push a last cup of rakshi into our hands.

When we were able to begin the hike up the steep trail out of the village, everyone in the village except the elders and matriarchs joined us for the hike up to the trailhead. The band led the way with their drums thumping out a marching beat and the flutes blowing a triumphal tune. Children held our hands and clung to our arms and sides. They really did not want us to leave.

It seemed to me that there is such a high level of emotional security in the community that villagers expressed openly and unhesitatingly their feelings about our departure—sadness. It was an intensely bittersweet parting.

I have never experienced anything so touching in all my travel experiences. Carl and Karen expressed similar sentiments when we were later able to talk about the experience. Eight months later, in June 2009, when Carl and I gave a program for the Central Indiana Wilderness Club about the trek to Basa, Carl told me he was still trying to process the experience. It was extraordinary to be treated like celebrities, and wonderfully gratifying to experience so much appreciation from the entire village for our work to improve the school. But it was more than the thrill of being the object of attention and recipient of the villagers' gratitude. The emotional honesty of the villagers was so powerfully affecting. To experience such warmth and sweetness from an entire community—little tykes, village elders and matriarchs, and across all of the castes—has had a powerful and lasting effect on the three of us.

Karen, Carl, and I did not want to leave Basa, but we had to make it to Phaplu that night. It was already late morning, and we had a hike ahead of us that had taken us a day and a half on the way in. How could we make it back to Phaplu by that evening, leaving Basa after ten in the morning?

21

BASA MAGNETISM

We stopped at the top of the ridge where the side trail cuts off from the main trail and leads down to Basa. We took one last look at the magical village. After more good-byes, the band, still thumping and tooting, led the adults back down the trail to the village. Most of the kids lingered with us at the overlook above the village. They wanted to hike with us to Phaplu. It was heart-rending to convince them to turn around and go back home. One little guy with droopy drawers clung to the friendly Yeti's hand. The little fellow would have been happy to let Carl stuff him in his backpack and tote him down the trail. Tears rolled down Toulashea's cheeks when she finally let go of Karen's hand. She stood in the middle of the trail crying as we turned our backs on the children of Basa and headed toward Phaplu.

We had to make time. Arjun, Sanga, Carl, Karen, and I started up the trail back to Sombare together but moving at a rapid pace, probably the fastest Karen had hiked on the trek. We hiked by the Himalayan Secondary School in Sombare that Ganesh and Sanga had attended as youngsters. Sanga told us that he and Ganesh had been best friends as boys and had hiked to school with each other every day. It was at school in Sombare that they decided they wanted to have lives outside of Basa 6.

Sanga leading Carl and his little buddy

Sanga said that he and Ganesh had dreamed of going to Kat-mandu. They eventually realized that the only way out of village life was to develop their language skills, especially English, and hire on to an expedition company. Sanga said they were lucky that Niru succeeded in his efforts to develop his own company. Ganesh and Sanga both married sisters of Niru and became two of his best sirdars. Ganesh had gone on to college, but, as he told me during one of our talks hiking together, there were so few opportunities in Nepal outside of farming and tourism that his college degree didn't open any other doors. Sanga confided to me that he would really like to start his own trekking company but didn't think it was likely to happen. So many new tour com-panies had started in Nepal when the trekking industry took off in the '90s that there was too much competition now and many companies were not making any money. Niru allowed Sanga to lead his own tours in Katmandu, and Sanga hoped to develop that business, but doubted he would be able to do much business on his own beyond the occasional day tour Niru referred to him.

Both Sanga and Ganesh, although they had each developed greater ambitions, were very grateful to Niru for the opportunity to live with him part of the year in Katmandu and travel throughout the Himalayas guiding expeditions. Yet, like Niru, they loved their village. Unlike Niru, their homes and families were still in Basa. Sanga told me that Nanda would never leave Basa to live in Katmandu. Sanga thinks most of the villagers, especially the women, would not be happy living in a city. He said, "For most people, the village side is better. They become confused and lose their way in Katmandu."

As we passed the Himalayan Secondary School, we saw students practicing dancing in the schoolyard. Sanga stopped and gazed at the sight. He smiled reflectively and said his favorite part of the school day when he was a kid had been the singing and dancing class.

Since Sanga was into reminiscing about his school days, I asked if he'd like to stop at the school. I'm sure all of us would have enjoyed it, but we had to make tracks to Phaplu. He shook his head and we pushed on, picking up the pace.

As we hiked through Sombare, Sanga and I talked about how education of the village children would affect the culture of Basa. I asked whether he recognized that providing a more Western-style education for the kids would bring change to the village. My point was that these children, even with just a fifth grade education, would think thoughts their parents never thought and would develop curiosity about the outside world. They would then likely want to leave Basa to experience or join the more urban and modern world.

Sanga's response was pretty much the same as the Sherpas I had interviewed in 2003 about changes within their communities from modernization. He saw only benefit for the students and teachers from the modern educational materials I had brought and from the materials my friend John Moreland would be shipping from the Indiana Department of Education. Sanga did not agree that improving the school or, for that matter, bringing modern conveniences to Basa could be a curse; in his view, it would only be a blessing.

I asked Sanga how he felt about bringing more trekkers to Basa. He was thrilled with the idea, and hoped Basa could become a tourist destination. He did not share my fear that tourism would facilitate loosening the bonds of the traditional ways and pushing the village down the slide toward modern consumer culture. Although he understood why I thought modernism had made the Khumbu a less desirable destination, because it had lost some of the traditional Sherpa character that originally attracted me; Sanga, like my Sherpa friends, did not think his village would lose its unique character.

I felt like a lone voice crying in the wilderness. My Nepalese friends do not see the possibility, to me the inevitability, of the domino effect of introducing the modern world into the delicate balance of a harmonious Himalayan village culture. Why would Basa be different from villages in the Khumbu? What is to protect it from losing its equilibrium to consumer acquisitiveness?

Perhaps I was laying a guilt trip on myself, worrying too much about how I might be responsible for starting a cascading effect that would infect the beautiful flower of Basa with consumerism. But I was worried, because the little community is such a delightful place the way it is. And not to recognize my own responsibility is to be like the lawyer who tries to get the guilty defendant off and rationalizes it by claiming, "If I don't take the case, some other lawyer will." I am the one Niru has asked to help develop

Basa. So it is my responsibility to determine whether that is the right thing for me to do.

In support of Niru's view that education and modern conveniences such as electricity and water will be good for Basa, the defense should offer Niru, Ganesh, and Sanga as Exhibits A, B, and C. These are men who have been exposed to the modern world and have, to a significant extent, adopted its ways. They wear modern clothes, use the Internet, and follow international affairs. Yet they are truly fine human beings and have retained the unique character of strength, gentleness, and compassion that I so admire in Himalayan highlanders. They also return to Basa and live in Basa, just like the other villagers, and they support its traditions and community.

Exhibit D is Nanda Kumari Rai, Sanga's wife. She is an educated woman who wants to provide the children of Basa with a better education than she received. Yet she wears traditional dress, maintains her household in the traditional ways, and has no desire to leave "the village side." In addition to raising her own little boy, she is caring for eight orphaned children and is the principal of the school. Her life is devoted to the community of Basa, particularly its children. Sanga told me that what Nanda longs for, and works for, is to provide the children of Basa with an education that will help them to learn to be more than farmers.

But to what end? If there is no opportunity for the children of Basa other than subsistence farming, one might argue that the kids would be better off without an education.

Is Niru's case for the economic development of Basa proven? If improvement in the standard of living is what the case is about, yes, he wins. But I cannot let go of my fears about the long-term effects on the community. Despite my misgivings, perhaps my role is to trust the people I have come to know and admire, and to try to help in the ways they ask for help. I know the future is not truly inevitable. The domino effect is not a certainty. There must be a future for the children of Basa whether it is in the village side or in the city side.

I pushed these thoughts to the back of my mind to be revisited later. We had to push on to Phaplu.

As we turned away from the Sombare school to resume hiking, Sanga remarked that village children would have to find a way to support themselves and their families other than farming because the farms can't support everyone now that families are bigger. There wasn't time to pursue this point, so I filed it in my memory. But a light was beginning to turn on in my mind.

Troubles on the Trail

The hike back to the suspension bridge high over the Kaku Khola went well. We kept up a fast pace as the trail had minimal altitude gain. But on the other side of the bridge was the 11,000-foot Ratnagi Danda. Karen was doing okay, but her pace began to slow as we approached the bridge. Before crossing the bridge, we took a short break to eat the sack lunches Purna had prepared for us. It was pleasant to eat a fresh apple and spam sandwich in the shade. It was getting hot as the sun climbed higher in the cloudless sky.

After we crossed the suspension bridge, I decided I would strike out ahead of Karen, Carl, Sanga, and Arjun. I could see our porters moving in a line up a steep trail on the other side of the bridge, working their way up to the pass over Ratnagi Danda. I set off to catch them.

I legged it as fast as I could and after about an hour caught up to the seven porters carrying our duffels and the company's tents and kitchen gear back to Phaplu. The guys were taking a break under some shade trees. They were still feeling high from time at home and having an easy job carrying relatively light loads.

Bhaktu Rai, one of the older and stronger men in the crew, and I had joked around about our different dietary habits. My description of his and the other porters' daily meals was "bhat, bhat, and bhat" (rice, rice, and rice). He made jokes about the way Westerners eat, mimicking the dainty use of a knife and fork. The other porters thought his pantomime was hilarious. We went through our comedy routine about our differing diets one last time. I shared the last of my stash of granola bars with Bhaktu and the other guys. It was the last day on the trail, so I wouldn't need the extra snacks. Every porter I know likes granola bars, even from a Westerner who just made fun of their all-rice diet.

When we finished our granola bar snacks, we could see Sanga and Carl on a different trail below us and Karen and Arjun trailing them. Sanga waved his arms, beckoning me to come down to the lower trail. The porters hoisted their dokos and started walking on up the higher trail. I was confused and didn't understand why Sanga wanted me to come down to the lower trail, but I spent fifteen minutes working my way back down. By the time I had backtracked far enough to scramble over a ledge and jump down to the lower trail, Arjun and Karen were just ahead, waiting for me. Sanga and Carl were well ahead of us.

Karen was flushed and said she did not feel well. She looked weak, even though Arjun was carrying her pack. I asked if she was hydrating. She said she was, and had already drunk most of her water. There was only a little water left in her second bottle. Arjun had some left in his, and said he would share with Karen. He also told us we would be able to get water from some of the farm settlements we would pass farther up the trail. It was a hot day, around 90 degrees Fahrenheit and humid.

I asked why Sanga wanted me to come back down to the lower trail. Arjun explained that the porters were taking a shortcut that would be "too hard for us," by which I assumed he meant too hard for Karen. Apparently, Sanga wanted Karen, Carl, and me to stay with him and Arjun on the easier but longer trail back to Phaplu.

I hiked with Karen and Arjun a little way but became increasingly impatient because Karen was so slow. It was as if she were dragging a piano behind her. She had started off well in the morning but was now slower than she had been since the first day when her feet were so terribly blistered. We would have to hike uphill all day to reach the top of the pass over the 11,000-foot Ratnagi Danda. Karen was struggling hard up the steep trail; she had to stop every few yards to catch her breath and try to loosen the tightening muscles in her upper legs.

Carl and Sanga were out of sight around a few bends ahead on the trail winding around the huge flank of the Ratnagi Danda. I set off to catch up with them. After I was out of sight of Arjun and Karen, I came to a trail fork and assumed I should take the high path. After hiking that trail for about half an hour, I caught up to Carl and Sanga, but they were on a different trail below me. Sanga whistled and waved his arms signaling for me to go back and come down to the lower trail. I yelled and gestured, trying to ask if I couldn't just meet them at the top of the pass. I couldn't understand what he yelled back as we were too far away and the great space made by the ridge and huge river valley carried his voice away from me. But I could see him shaking his head and waving me back down.

God damn it, I was mad! I cursed and muttered. Instead of hiking back down the trail to the fork, I scrambled down the steep hillside, jumping and tripping over rocks and scrubby brush. I was furious that I had lost another half-hour or more and used up valuable energy. I was now almost out of water and was sweating profusely as I scrambled off trail down the ridge. I was pissed off that I had not just ignored Sanga and hung with the porters on their shortcut back to Phaplu. I stumbled into a farmer's barley field. The family was working the field and two daughters, a son, and father stared at me like I was an apparition as I stomped through their field, bowing and saying "namaste" as I passed them.

I felt like a fool and had let go of most of my anger and irritation by the time I found the low trail again. We are not at our best when physically or psychologically stressed. I felt ashamed that I had not been more sympathetic to Bill.

Sanga and Carl had hiked on, but here again were Karen and Arjun slowly inching their way up the trail. They were out of water, and Karen looked even worse. I was worried she would get dehydrated and not be able to make it up to the pass. Looking up, it appeared we might be halfway to reaching the pass and it was mid afternoon. I gave Karen the little bit of water I had left. Arjun walked over to the barley field and yelled at the farm family, asking if they had water we could take. A didi came out of the house and conferred with Arjun. He walked back to us and reported that there was no water here, but we could get water farther up the trail. So we pushed on.

Arjun and I tried to keep up a cheerful patter, hoping to help keep Karen's spirits up. She didn't say much as she plodded doggedly up the trail. She did say that she felt terribly heavy. She said it felt like she was carrying fifty extra pounds. She looked kind of scared. She said she thought some force was pulling her back down the trail, and she had to fight it every step. It sounded a little crazy to me, and I worried that she was getting dehydrated and loopy. But the way she was moving did look like she was struggling against some force other than gravity resisting her upward progress.

I decided I better stay with Karen and Arjun. We moved slowly, slowly up the steep dusty and rocky trail with unforgiving heat from the sun beating down on us. Phaplu was west of us, so as the afternoon wore on and we made our slow progress up the side of the mountain, we were climbing into the sun. The heat and glare were unremitting and we were out of water.

But joy! A one-room bhatti with a hose line fed by a mountain stream appeared beside the trail within an hour of our last drink of water. We gratefully poured water over our heads. Karen soaked her shirt with water. I was shirtless, so I drenched my upper body. Arjun just grinned at us, and then shook the water out of his thick black hair like a dog shaking water off its fur. He got a weak laugh out of Karen.

The old didi who ran the bhatti told Arjun that Sanga and Carl had stopped there an hour ago. We filled our bottles and set off.

Karen was a little stronger after quenching her thirst but soon fell back to her painfully slow pace. I walked in front but kept looking over my shoulder to make sure I wasn't moving too quickly for Karen. Arjun brought up the rear, with an easy swinging stride, carrying his big pack on his back and Karen's daypack in front.

Karen started talking to herself and shaking her head. I couldn't understand what she was saying, so I stopped and asked what was going on with her. There was fear in her eyes. At first she shook her head, like she wasn't going to say anything, but then speaking in a low tone she said she understood what was happening to her. She called it "Basa magnetism." She said Basa was exerting a powerful magnetic force on her and it was trying to pull her back. Karen said she could feel this force physically restraining her, but she called it a spiritual force. The spirit of Basa had a hold on her.

It was freaky, but it made a strange, mystical sense. There was obviously something at work, which was weakening her and making it much more difficult than it should have been for Karen to hike up the trail and out of the valley away from Basa. I looked at Arjun, like maybe he could offer some other explanation. He smiled kindly at me and nodded that we should move on. He seemed unfazed by Karen's revelation, as if he'd seen it before or, at least, understood the spirit force of Basa magnetism.

After trudging upward, ever upward, for another couple of hours, we ran out of water again. Arjun and I kept up our happy talk, trying to encourage Karen to keep going. She smiled weakly at our jokes. Since joking around wasn't helping much, Arjun and I tried singing. We serenaded Karen with the one Nepali folk song I know, "Resham Phiri Ri." It didn't seem to help. Karen looked flushed, dehydrated, and kind of blank.

A water fountain appeared like a mirage beside the trail ahead of us. Arjun must have known it was there, but I did not remember it from our descent the day before. Just a day ago! It seemed we had experienced so much more than one day could contain.

The fountain, by a farm settlement at a bend in the trail, overlooks a 2,000—3,000 foot drop-off. It reminded me of a scene from an old B movie of explorers dying of thirst in the desert and seeing the mirage of a lake appearing in the middle of the desert. But it was real. The fountain had underground plumbing with a tap, concrete base, and drain, and a dedication inscription from a Swiss NGO. Karen and I doused ourselves and filled our water bottles again. Arjun drank a little. He was only mildly thirsty.

The shadow created by the sun dropping behind the ridge above us was creeping down the side of the mountain toward us. It would be a relief to hike in shade, but then darkness would not be far behind. We seemed to be closing in on the pass above us, but it was as hard to see now that it was shaded as it had been trying to look into the glare of the bright sun earlier in the day. I knew Karen would be safe with Arjun, so I told them I was going to hike on ahead and try to catch up with Carl and Sanga. I said I'd wait for them at the top of the pass, and began hiking fast and hard up the steep trail.

I couldn't see Carl or Sanga. They were hidden by scrub pine, which appeared in patches in the upper portion of the ridge. I caught up to them about thirty minutes later. I told them Arjun and Karen were not too far behind but that Karen was really struggling. They told me they had stopped and waited at the bhatti for us, but moved on when they became concerned about getting to Phaplu before nightfall. We agreed we would wait for Karen and Arjun at the top of the pass, and started hiking again.

I asked Sanga why he had called me down the second time from the higher trail. He explained that that particular trail ended at a settlement high on the ridge and didn't go over the pass to Phaplu. I conceded he'd done me a favor. He also told me I wouldn't like the trail the porters took because it went across several streams and I would "get wet." I was no longer upset, so I didn't argue the point, but I couldn't help thinking it would have been a better experience to hike with Bhaktu, Dhruba, Mati, and the other porters even if it required getting wet.

The top of the great ridge seemed to keep receding from us. Each time I looked up and thought I could see the top, it was no closer than the last time I looked up. The shadow descending from the crest of the ridge enveloped us as we were hiking through pine and rhododendrons. Finally, the temperature began to drop. Since I was no longer sweating under a glaring sun, I felt stronger. I sped up and left Sanga and Carl behind.

When I reached the top of the pass, I would have jumped for joy, but there was no spring left in my legs. About ten minutes later, Sanga came running up over the crest with a worried look on his face. He said he had been yelling for me to stop at the pass, because he was afraid I would take the wrong trail again. He said, "I tried to catch you, but long legs go faster than short legs!" We both laughed and clasped each other on the shoulders.

There were three different trails running off the pass in a westerly direction toward Phaplu. Sanga asked which one I thought was the Phaplu trail. I remembered it was the one to our far right, which Sanga said was the correct answer. So the one time I would have chosen the right trail that day, I waited instead of striking off on my own.

Carl arrived a short time later. He had kept a steady pace the whole day, but he was very gassed by the time he crested the pass. He slumped down against the mani wall marking the Phurlung Pass and quietly entered a meditative state. He perked up when a mother and her son walked up, plopped down on their haunches, and eyed him curiously. The boy spoke some English. Carl engaged them in conversation and we were soon trading uneaten cookies and boiled eggs from our sack lunches for dried fruit and roti with our new friends.

We waited about forty-five minutes for Karen and Arjun. Carl was concerned, as was I, about hiking after dark on the slippery roller-coaster stretch of trail where Dax had bailed. Sanga agreed we should hike on to Phaplu. We were sure Karen would be safe with Arjun.

About fifteen minutes after we started down the trail from the top, we heard Karen and Arjun behind us, laughing gleefully.

Carl resting by mani stones on top of Phurlung Pass

We stopped and waited. They came hauling ass down the trail like a couple of kids on a sugar buzz. Karen literally skipped up to us, looking the picture of health.

I was astounded. Before I could ask for an explanation, Karen, in a rush of words, said that as she neared the top of the pass, the force pulling her back began to lessen, and when she reached the crest of the ridge, the force released her. She felt fine. In fact, she felt great.

She turned to Carl and Sanga and explained that after we left the village she began to feel this magnetic-like force trying to pull her back to Basa. It got stronger during the long climb up Ratnagi Danda, but then released her at the top. She said she thought it was a spiritual power trying to tell her she shouldn't leave Basa. She promised the spirit she would return. During her cascade of words, Arjun stood behind her smiling sweetly and nodding along with everything Karen said.

There was no time to dwell on the meaning of Karen's encounter with the spirit world. Dusk was approaching. So we hurried down the trail at a brisk pace, trotting when we could. But this was the slippery up-and-down stage that had so discomfited Dax two days ago. Now it was muddy as well as slippery. There were several steep downhills, which we tried to schuss down using our trekking poles like ski poles. Our trekking boots were covered in mud and soaked with water as we splashed through puddles and across streams. So much for not getting wet.

Each of us, even Sanga and Arjun, slipped a few times. But when Carl started to go down, he was like a great sequoia falling; there was no stopping him from hitting the ground. He fell several times and his left side, from knee to shoulder was smeared with mud. His good humor held, and he got up laughing or grinning each time, until about the fifth tumble. He hoisted himself up and said tight-jawed, "That's it! I'm not going to fall again." About five minutes later, he fell again. We all, Carl included, laughed giddily.

Karen was the giddiest. And she was jetting along faster than any of us. It was hard to keep up with her. The transformation was incredible; but there she was, whipping down the trail, jumping streams, and schussing down mud hills. A couple of hours before, she looked half dead in her boots.

Sundown had come just after six every night on the trek. But strangely, the night of October 15, 2008, as we hiked to Phaplu, it seemed as though time was suspended. Dusk came as we hiked through the roller-coaster stretch of trail, but it remained dusk. It did not become dark. Visibility remained in a dusky transition state for several hours, and it was still not dark when we arrived at the Number Lodge in Phaplu.

Our trek was over.

Arjun, Karen, Carl, Sanga, and me (right to left)
at Number Lodge, Phaplu

22

NIGHT IN PHAPLU

Bhaktu, Dhruba, Mati, and the rest of the porters had, not surprisingly, arrived before us at the Number Lodge. Our three tents were set up in a field behind the lodge with our duffels inside the tents. It wasn't a bad campsite, except for a couple of mangy dogs grouchily patrolling the grounds and an ample supply of cow patties to step over.

We had burned a ton of calories during the long hike up the Ratnagi Danda, and we were in dire need of nourishment. After checking out the tents and duffels, we stumped into the lodge. Since Purna stayed at home in Basa, Sanga told us to order anything we wanted on the lodge's menu for dinner. Carl, Karen, and I sat in a small banquet room by ourselves. By the time we ate dinner, the other guests in the lodge had gone to bed. I think Carl had Sherpa stew, and I ordered spaghetti; yes, spaghetti was on the menu. Whatever Karen ordered, she didn't eat it. She picked at her food but had no appetite. To celebrate the last night of the trek, Sanga and Arjun somehow rustled up a chocolate cake. But our celebratory mood evaporated.

The high Karen had been on when she came over the pass had disappeared. As soon as we sat down to eat, she began to look pale again and her mood became desultory. For some reason, the topic of Hurricane Katrina came up during dinner. Karen became very agitated and then got uncharacteristically angry with Carl and me when she misunderstood our interest in discussing policy issues as a lack of sympathy for the victims of the hurricane. Katrina hit Karen's hometown (Biloxi, Mississippi) hard and many friends and acquaintances of Karen had lost homes and businesses. The hurricane was in 2005, three years before our trek, but Carl and I had obviously touched a still-raw nerve by offering up in rather neutral, clinical terms our opinions and analyses of the government's inadequate response. Karen lost her temper and yelled at us, basically calling Carl and me unsympathetic bastards who couldn't understand what it meant to live through a horrible experience like Katrina. It was totally unlike her, and Carl and I lapsed into stunned and embarrassed silence.

After venting at us for a while, Karen apologized and said she was getting sick and just needed to go to bed. She asked Sanga to arrange for a room in the lodge. She felt too ill to deal with her gear in the tent. I wondered if she might be dehydrated.

Carl and I finished eating while Sanga and Arjun checked Karen into a room and then brought her duffel to the room. Carl moseyed off to his tent. I took the opportunity of purchasing for the equivalent of a dollar the luxury of a shower in the lodge. Like most Sherpa lodges developed in the 1980s or later, the shower room was a closet with a concrete floor and drain in the center of the floor. The shower was a rusted pipe connected to a barrel of water with a kerosene heater. But the water was warm, and it was my one and only shower since leaving Katmandu a week ago. It was well worth the dollar.

After finishing the shower, I put on my long johns under my clothes as the temperature was still dropping. I wanted to look in on Karen on my way back to the tent. Her room was down a darkened hall in the lodge. I had to turn on my headlamp to find my way. Boards creaked underfoot. The door to Karen's room was open. Sanga and Arjun stood beside the bed and turned to me with looks of concern on their faces.

Karen was hugging herself and shaking in her sleeping bag on the bed. She turned to me and said she was hypothermic and had asked Arjun to get in the bed and share his body heat, but that he was either too shy or didn't understand what she wanted. I looked at Sanga, and he spoke up nervously, "It's okay, it's okay. Karen, she has the hypothermia." Sanga had filled Karen's water bottle with warm water, and she had taken Diomox, but she was still shivering. Her core temperature must have dropped precipitously after we arrived at the lodge. She had been sedentary for a couple of hours after hiking under the hot sun all day. Karen's system simply crashed that night after the most physically and spiritually challenging day of her life.

I asked Arjun if he wouldn't mind helping to warm up Karen by hugging her. He smiled shyly and backed out of the room. I got in the sleeping bag and wrapped my arms around her. She thanked me. Sanga backed out of the room, nodding all the way, and discretely closed the door behind him. Karen giggled and said, "They're so cute when they're shy." I held her close for about twenty minutes, and started to fall asleep. She elbowed me in the ribs and told me I better go off to bed before I fell asleep on her. She thanked me for being such a good friend. She said she would be fine now. I squeezed her shoulder and walked out of the lodge to my tent in the chill air. I could see my breath with each exhalation. It was after midnight, but the sky was so lit up with stars I didn't need to turn on my headlamp to find the tent.

Carl's tent glowed from a light inside, so I surmised he was awake and reading. I called to him and he answered. After I crawled into my sleeping bag, Carl and I chatted for a while before we each dozed off. I told him about Karen's hypothermia, and he said he knew something must have been wrong with her because she was so unlike herself at dinner. We laughed at the weirdness of the coincidence that Bill was hypothermic the first night in Deorali and Karen the last night in Phaplu. And we marveled at the amazing highs and lows Karen had hit in the last twenty-four hours. Carl said he didn't know how to process the whole experience—not just Basa, but all of Nepal. He said he had been affected so deeply in unexpected ways, he just didn't know how to deal with it. We left it at that.

◌ ▣ ◙ ◌ ▣

I woke up once during the night and struggled out of my sleeping bag and tent to pee. A couple of water buffalos had come into our campsite and were snuffling around the tents. Carl was snoring.

I stood outside the tent in the darkness. The white peak of Mount Number glowed in the starlight. This was my last night in the mountains for the year 2008. Being in the Himalayas inspires wonder, humbleness, and a quieting of the soul. I didn't want it to end.

Zipped up back in my bag, I lay quietly, enjoying the night sounds. Carl's snoring blended with the cows snuffling in a sort of timbrel melody. It was not the music of the spheres, but it was an oddly pleasant accompaniment to the poetic turn of mind I was experiencing.

It had been an incredible day. I had never experienced the warmth and appreciation of a community like we did in Basa. And I had never experienced a community so beautifully integrated as Basa. So what to make of the effect on Karen? Her spiritual or psychological connection to Basa was so deep, it had felt to her that her body was gripped by a force trying to prevent her from leaving. Maybe it was the power of the love of the children like Toulashea for her and her response to them. Karen said several times she wished she could adopt a child like Toulashea. Maybe it was a spirit or demon. Whatever it was it had played hell with her mind and body. Perhaps it was a warning from the spirit world to us that there is a cost to outsiders for messing with a community like Basa. It would not be only Basa that would be in jeopardy from our contact with it.

In a village like Basa, individuation takes a back seat to community. Individual expression is allowed and encouraged to some extent. Women express themselves through their jewelry, men wear different clothes, and families display their prosperity through the lushness of their thangra and collection of bronze trays. But survival depends on cooperation. If there is not a cooperative system in place, the dangerous and powerful forces of nature will destroy the village.

The harmonious equilibrium of such a tightly knit community creates energy like a centripetal force. The force that holds the community together can be threatened by outside influences such as exposure to consumer culture. But the force pulls people into community and tries to hold them in Basa. That is why Niru has not completely left the village; it has a hold on him. Sanga and Ganesh still make their homes there, despite their cultural sophistication. It won't let them go. And it pulled in the Chettri teacher who came to Basa to teach Nepali, along with the teacher's family.

Karen tapped into the power of the centripetal force of Basa. She called it Basa magnetism. I felt it too. I already wanted to go back.

23

OUT OF THE MOUNTAINS

Bhaktu, Dhruba, and Mati appeared like clockwork, and for the last time, at our tents in the morning to wake us and carry our duffels down to the airstrip. The field behind the lodge was wet with dew and it was still chilly enough that washing at a trough outside was bracing. Sanga came out of the lodge and reminded us we would eat breakfast in the lodge and then walk down to the airport for the flight back to Katmandu.

The previous night before dinner, Sanga told us he had learned from the lodge's staff that Bill had arrived at the Number Lodge the day after we had been in Phaplu. Bill, Dax, and David had flown to Katmandu the day we were in Basa. We would see our three compatriots back in Katmandu.

Bhaktu, Dhruba, and Mati guarded our duffels at the Phaplu airstrip while Arjun, Sanga, Karen, Carl, and I ate breakfast at the lodge. When we arrived at the airport, they lined up and bowed to each of us in the traditional acknowledgment of re-spect. Karen, Carl, and I responded in kind, and then we each hugged them in the less traditional Western way. Sanga gave the three porters instructions and off they walked. They would be back in Basa before nightfall

Arjun, Sanga, Carl, Karen, and I spent most of the morning waiting for the prop plane to fly into Phaplu from Katmandu.

Karen, Carl, and I were the only "white people" waiting for the plane. The little terminal was cramped and not air-conditioned. The five of us sat outside under a shade tree, leaning against a boulder just off the dirt runway. We killed time reminiscing about the past week and telling stories of other travels. Arjun cracked open some type of shelled nuts and passed them around.

I told the others about an experience I'd had in the island nation of Palau.

Kayaking Alone in the Dark

After getting blown off Mera Peak and thinking I was done with the Himalayas, I solo-kayaked in the Rock Islands of Palau for the first time in 2001. My plan was to paddle from Koror to Jellyfish Lake and back, camping out on the islands by myself for four or five days.

By 5:00 p.m. the second day of paddling, I was wearing out from pulling against two- to three-foot swells and fighting the tidal current. I had been paddling since nine in the morning, except for a two-hour lunch break and nap on an island beach. At five, there was only an hour of sunlight left in the day and I needed to find a campsite. I was gassed.

I was bothered both by doubt and weariness. It had been cloudy and misty all afternoon; as sundown approached, visibility was getting worse. The closer I got to Eil Malk, the island of Jellyfish Lake, the less sure I was that I knew which point of land I was supposed to track to find the inlet to the dock below Jellyfish Lake. On the map, Eil Malk looks like three fingers extending north from the palm of a hand, but with small rock islands sprinkled all around the fingers. In the misty dimness of early evening, I wasn't sure which points of land were fingers of Eil Malk and which were rock islands.

As I started down what I hoped was the mile-long inlet to the Jellyfish Lake dock, the sun began to set. I hadn't planned on paddling in the dark. I don't like paddling after dark, not even on my own White River back home in Indiana. The moon had been full the last few nights, but that night, clouds blotted out the moonlight. I paddled for an hour and the land on my left disappeared in the darkness. Not because of the darkness, but because it was a long rock island I had mistaken for the outer finger of Eil Malk. I could hear the surf breaking on the outer reef as the vast grayness of the Pacific and the darkness of the sky enveloped everything to my left. The lights of a freighter moving slowly toward Koror blinked through the darkness miles away.

I could make out the tree line on my right and could clearly hear the slap of waves against the limestone wall of the Pacific side of Eil Malk. I cradled the paddle on my knees, opened a dry bag, and got out a headlamp. I scanned the shore for a place to beach the kayak, but there wasn't any. The Pacific side of Eil Malk was a sheer limestone wall. Dense mangrove jungle covered what little of the island I could see above and beyond the six-foot rock wall. I paddled onward, desperate to find a place I could beach the kayak and rest.

After paddling for two more hours, I glimpsed a white spot in the dimness ahead and paddled toward it. The white spot took the shape of a thirty-foot fishing boat half sunk on its port side with waves slapping against its hull. A small beach was visible just beyond the sunken hulk. Happily, I steered past the white hull and rode the waves onto the beach.

As I pulled the kayak onto the sand, my joy quickly dissolved. There was less than twenty feet of sand between the water line and impenetrably dense vegetation. It was past seven in the evening, but high tide wouldn't crest until about nine. Within an hour, there wouldn't be any beach left. It would be underwater before high tide peaked.

I considered tying the kayak to the trunk of a palm tree, and riding out the high tide in the kayak. But I was afraid the wave action would roll the kayak and tumble my gear and me into the surf. Louder than the slap of waves on sand was an eerie groaning noise coming from the half-sunken boat. It sounded like the wheezing of an ancient bellows or the death rattle of some giant monster. The mournful groaning of the white hulk was too much; I retied gear onto the kayak. Although I felt weak in the knees, I pushed the loaded kayak back into the surf. All I could think to do was to try to paddle back to where I missed the turn for Jellyfish Lake.

Heading north, I could hear the surf breaking on the outer reef fifty or sixty yards to my right. I could see a dim outline of trees and could hear the slap of waves on the rock wall of Eil Malk on my left. I had to steer a course between the surf breaking on the outer reef and the waves smacking the wall at the base of the island. I was scared and crying and cursing myself for my navigational stupidity and the perversity that would take me from hearth and home to be paddling a kayak by myself in the Pacific Ocean at night! Worst of all, I was now totally exhausted.

I simply did not have the physical reserves required to make the hard two hours of paddling back to the turn I had missed and another mile down the inlet to the safety of Jellyfish Lake dock. Suddenly, I felt something bump the bottom of the kayak, and shark terror entered the mix of roiling emotion, recrimination, and exhaustion. My arms were trembling from the exertion of pulling through three-foot waves against a head wind. My chest was heaving as my lungs tried to replenish my spent muscles with oxygen. My heart was pounding with fear—fear that I could not continue paddling for two hours and fear that the kayak would tip and I would be in the dark water alone, like Jonah, with the monster that bumped the bottom of the boat.

I stopped paddling, rested the paddle on my lap, and tried to control my breathing and calm myself. The kayak rose and fell with the rolling waves. I started singing two hymns I had sung in church every Sunday when I was a small child pressed warmly against the side of my great-grandmother in the hard wooden pews of our little church in Goshen, Indiana: *Gloria Patri* and "The Doxology."

Glory be to the Father, and to the Son, and to the Holy Ghost;
As it was in the beginning, is now and ever shall be,
World without end; A-men, A—men

Praise God from whom all blessings flow;
Praise God, all creatures here below;
Praise God above, ye heavenly host;
Praise Father, Son, and Holy Ghost.

I had learned to chant Buddhist mantras on mountaineering expeditions in the Himalayas. Chanting a mantra frees the mind of nervous energy, allows the body to move spontaneously, and takes one out of time to reduce the drudgery of a long trek or climb. On the ocean alone that night, I applied what I'd learned in the mountains, but used the Christian mantras of my childhood. The panicky buzzing in my mind began to ebb, the tightness in my muscles relaxed, and I let go of the abuse I'd heaped on myself. My troubled spirit calmed and a renewed strength energized my muscles. I felt like I could paddle all night long.

Ninety minutes later, as I rounded the point I'd earlier missed, the clouds opened like a theater curtain being drawn back. The moon made its first appearance of the evening, lighting up mangrove roots overhanging the limestone edge of the island, and shimmering on the surface of the rippling water. As I entered the inlet to Jellyfish Lake, it felt like two arms of Eil Malk embraced me. The water in the inlet was as calm as a pond in Indiana. I was lost and, by what seemed like an amazing grace, I was safe. I straddled the kayak with my legs and let my feet dangle over the sides in the water, while I slowly paddled the last half-mile to the dock below Jellyfish Lake.

I told the others the story of the amazing grace I experienced on the ocean in Palau because that experience was the closest parallel I had to what we had experienced in Basa. There had been great physical challenge beyond the expected, stress, and fear, but a singular and unforgettable experience as the ultimate reward. On the ocean, I had been alone. The experience of Basa was shared with companions and given to us by an entire community.

There was magnetism in both places. I returned to Palau two more times in the next three years and solo-paddled to Jellyfish Lake again and farther throughout the Rock Islands. That place has a mystical hold on me and I will go back again. I told Karen and Carl that the pull of Basa that Karen felt so strongly hiking up Ratnagi Danda was not done with us. We would have to go back.

▫ ▪ ◉ ▫ ▪

After whiling away several hours by the airstrip, we finally heard the distant buzz that became a roar as the prop plane approached the landing strip. It was time for us to board and fly back to Katmandu.

It was especially difficult for Karen to let go of Arjun. We gave him a group hug and then left the two of them for a private moment before we had to run up the steps and choose seats in the plane.

The flight attendant handed out cotton balls to stuff into our ears and hard candy to chew to help our ears adjust to the diminishing pressure as we gained altitude, as is customary on domestic flights in Nepal. Nepalese of varying tribes and castes joined us in the twenty-seat Twin Otter. We watched as the ground crew tossed boxes, barrels, suitcases, and our duffels into the storage compartments in the underbelly and back of the plane. Several boxes of fresh eggs and two chickens in a little wooden crate occupied seats in the back. Then we were airborne and winging our way back to Katmandu.

We could see the great white caps of the High Himalayas just outside the windows on the right side of the plane. I told Carl and Karen to sit on that side to enjoy the views. Sanga and I sat on the left. The plane took us farther and farther away from Basa. In less than an hour, the green terraces of the Katmandu Valley came into view.

We had left Katmandu just eight days before. This trek gave me no more days and nights in the Himalayas than the introductory trek I had done in 1995, my first visit to Nepal. That first trek had changed my life. It was the beginning of my love for the mountains and the mountain people, the beginning of my journey toward making a commitment to create constructive engagement with Himalayan villages. In a sense, the Basa trek was the fulfillment of my pledge. At least two more Americans had fallen in love with Nepal and were transformed by their encounter with the Himalayas. The Basa School Project would be a success. The lives of the schoolchildren, and the entire village, I hoped, would be improved as a result.

But the Basa trek was also the beginning of a new chapter. I would have to go back. There was more to give, and more to receive.

24

BACK IN KATMANDU

At Tribhuvan Airport, we disembarked and crossed the baking tarmac. Sweating attendants threw our duffels, along with all the baggage in the plane, onto a creaking metal-wheeled cart. We followed the cart into the decrepit domestic terminal. The bags were sorted and Sanga directed us to stack our duffels onto two three-wheeled pushcarts. Sanga and I guided the carts out of the baggage area. The cart I was pushing had a rusted and sticky wheel. I had to wrestle the cart forward while the wheel squeaked and fought me as sweat soaked through my clothes.

Niru was waiting for us at the gate outside. He greeted each of us in the traditional way, bowing, with palms together, and smiled benignly as he asked if we had a good trek. Karen, Carl, and I made a chorus out of assuring Niru we had a great trek. Like the porter he used to be, Niru took the handle of my cart and muscled it through the parking lot, with Sanga pushing the other cart and the three of us following.

The van Niru had arranged took us to the Katmandu Guest House. The polluted air of narrow Katmandu streets choked with tuk-tuks, motorcycles, bicycles, cars, trucks, ancient chugging buses, pedestrians in colorful saris and topis, and the occasional cow or dog wandering into traffic blasted our senses with a mélange of bright colors and powerful odors. After a week in the mountains and small villages, driving through Katmandu was a shock to our mellowed-out consciousness. But, I suppose, it was a necessary beginning to the transition back into our "real world."

Uttam, my friend and KGH manager, greeted us upon our arrival and insisted we join him for tea and tell him about the trek. Bill, David, and Dax were rounded up, so our group was reunited for tea in the KGH outdoor restaurant, where we had spent much time before our departure for Jiri. Uttam listened with interest as we each shared our experiences of the last week. Karen, Carl, and I learned about Bill's teahouse trek with Some, and David and Dax's two days in Phaplu.

Dax and David had been bored in Phaplu. They told the rest of us that they got antsy sitting around the Number Lodge, so they set off on the mile hike down to the Solu government complex. David made it a few hundred yards before the pain in his groin became so intense he had to turn around and limp back to the lodge with Dax's help. After visiting the other "hotspots" on main street Phaplu that evening, they were ready to get out of town. They were relieved when Bill arrived so they could all fly back to Katmandu.

Dax and David said they became aware of Bill's entrance to the Number Lodge in Phaplu when they heard a loud American voice bellowing, "Meat! I want meat to eat!" This had immediately set their California sensitivity on edge, but they were able to laugh about it back in Katmandu. David said, "My reaction was, 'Oh, my God, the ugly American has arrived!'" Dax corrected him, "You mean the ugly Hoosier." I had to remind Dax again that Bill lives in California, and the three Californians were the ones who sat on their asses in Phaplu, while the two Hoosiers and the Mississippi belle trekked on to Basa and back.

Bill laughed too and said that he made Some find him meat twice each day as they trekked to Phaplu. It became a joke between them because Some never ate meat. Bill then related some surprising news. During his four days of hiking with Some, he said he had experienced a spiritual awakening. He had not become a Buddhist or Hindu, but his time on the trail had reinforced his own Christianity. He told us that his exposure to the hard life of Nepalese villagers had made him more appreciative of the bounty of his own life.

I was delighted to hear Bill relate that his experience in the mountains had given him a sense of greater spiritual enlightenment and, I hoped, cultural sensitivity. I had feared that the trek would be nothing but pain and suffering for him, and that he would leave Nepal regretting it as a painful experience and waste of time. But his time alone on the trail, his one-on-one relationship with Some, and his exposure to the local people and their simpler way of life had deeply impressed him. He was back to his natural gregarious self, but with a calmness that had been missing when he first arrived in Katmandu.

When Bill was able to trek at his own pace, the physical demand remained challenging but not so stressful that he was physically and emotionally trashed. Bill admitted he had not been able to handle the hard and fast pace when we were humping from Jiri to Deorali, and that he had become stressed out as well as overtaxed physically. When he was able to set his own hiking pace, his mind, body, and spirit relaxed.

In the van ride to Niru's house that evening for our farewell party, Bill excitedly elaborated on his trekking experience as a spiritual awakening. I understood the high he was on. I felt it, too, as I had after most of the expeditions I'd done. The first time I landed in Lukla, while we waited for our gear to be sorted off the chopper, I talked to a group of English and American trekkers who were ready to fly out after a successful trek to base camp and back. They were actually jumping up and down with glee; they were so jacked up from the high of trekking to the base of Chomolungma and back.

Whether the high carries forward into life after the trek is another question. The Harvard LSD experiments of the 1960s showed that, through the use of LSD, a subject could achieve an altered state of consciousness similar to that of a disciplined yogi engaged in meditative practice. The EEG-measured brain-wave patterns of the two states were similar. The "higher state" of consciousness attained through LSD use, however, was lost after the drug wore off and could not be recovered without use of the drug. A yogi, on the other hand, can return to a higher state of consciousness at will. A travel high is probably more like the former, likely to evaporate not long after the traveler returns to regular life. Still, even if the high is lost, the memories are not. I hoped Bill's memories would be enough to reinforce the spiritual enlightenment and greater sensitivity to cultural differences he described to me as we bumped along the rutted streets to Niru's house.

Farewell Party

At Niru's house on the outskirts of Katmandu, our group enjoyed a seven-course feast with Niru's family. Dax was being pissy and did not attend. But to my delight, Ganesh was in attendance, as was Sanga. Ganesh had returned from leading an expedition on Dhaulagiri. Although still buoyant, he bore the sad news of the death of a porter in his crew during the expedition. The cause of death was a heart attack.

Ganesh took me aside to share some of the depressing details. He said the porter was an older guy who was not from Basa. The gravity of the loss of a man's life and acceptance of such risks as natural to working in the mountains showed in Ganesh's expressive face.

When we sat down to begin the meal, many toasts were offered, especially to Sanga by Carl, Karen, and me for pushing us hard enough to get us to Basa for the extraordinary experience we had in the village. Of course, we all toasted and thanked Niru for putting the crew together and organizing the expedition. And we toasted and thanked Mrs. Niru for the splendid feast she served us.

Bill and Niru's oldest son, Milan, who works as the assistant manager of Adventure GeoTreks, made yak jokes throughout the evening. Bill even got down on the floor on all fours to imitate a water buffalo he'd seen, which he thought was a yak, walking up a steep trail. Bill was enjoying Mrs. Niru's rakshi as well as the San Miguel and Mount Everest beer she served. Before we left Niru's house, Bill and Milan had exchanged email addresses and Bill invited Milan to visit him in San Diego and, wink wink, hoped to introduce Milan to Bill's daughter.

While Bill and Milan were messing around, Sanga, David, and Karen reminisced about the trek. David performed a dead-on impression of Dax riffing on the gay bar he'd like to open in Phaplu to enliven Phaplu's nightlife.

Niru, Ganesh, Carl, and I weren't so cheery as we huddled to discuss Niru's request that I organize a fundraising drive to bring electricity to Basa. I saw this as my chance to discuss in person with three people I admire what Basa really needs and what would be the right way to share with Basa.

As I expected, my concern that there is a risk to Basa from too much exposure to Western ways, which might change the way of life of the village, made little impression on Niru and Ganesh. Carl sided with Niru and Ganesh but understood my fears about upsetting Basa's equilibrium.

Carl made two points. The first was that with sensitivity to the physical and social environment, hydroelectric power could be brought to the village with minimal damage and then the villagers could leapfrog forward to the 21st century in technology. After electricity, the next step would be to connect the village to the Internet, and then the villagers would be able to participate in the information economy without passing through a manufacturing-industrial phase. Carl's second point was that, if the village wants electricity and we are in a position to help bring it, who are we to decide for the local people that they should not have what they want? To deny Basa electricity in order to preserve it as a "museum," Carl argued, would be another form of Western paternalism.

Carl's arguments were compelling, to a degree, but my sense of foreboding about the fate of the village was not easily quelled. I had a hard time imagining the villagers plugged in and surfing the Net. This may be paternalistic thinking, but it didn't seem to me that bringing 21st-century technology to Basa would protect it from the disruptions to its community I feared.

It filled me with joy to know that Basa's children would have two more years of education—though I worry that they will develop curiosity about the outside world and the most curious will want to leave the village. But if that is what the children want, and that is what their parents want for them, should we not help make it happen, if we can?

If tourism comes to Basa, it may turn away from subsistence agriculture and toward a monetized commercial economy, just as the Khumbu Sherpas turned away from the yak as the center of their economy and made tourism the focus instead. The death of the porter on Ganesh's Dhaulagiri expedition, far from his village and family, reinforced the importance of the question: Are the Sherpas who now make their living from a commercial-tourist economy better off than those who continue to maintain the traditional way of life? Employment of villagers by Niru's company, Adventure GeoTreks, provides income necessary to purchase food when the produce grown in Basa runs out each year. Since Basa has no other employer, tourism through Adventure GeoTreks is what sustains the village and feeds its children. Yet, it also puts its men in danger.

On one of my kayaking expeditions in Palau, I shared a meal with a fisherman who lived in a house on the beach where I was camping. He marveled that I was kayaking for a week down the chain of islands that make up Palau. I pointed out that his ancestors had paddled boats similar to kayaks all across the Pacific Ocean. He laughed and said, "We Palauans are too lazy now. We have to use motors." Our conversation continued and he decried how Palauans have lost their traditional ways and become dependent on tourism and the U.S. government. About one-third of native Palauans are employed to do "make-work" for the government, which is financially supported by the U.S. government in exchange for military basing rights. Most of the others work in tourism and many get drunk and thrown in jail on Friday nights. Their native culture is at risk of dying. Obesity and alcoholism are rampant.

Palau looked like a paradise to Western visitors in the 19th and early 20th centuries. The local people were self-sufficient and lived very well off the bounty of the ocean and their taro crops. But during World War II, the Japanese occupied Palau and stayed until the Americans ousted them. Before the occupation, families and clans lived on the land communally without the concept of private property ownership. With the adoption of Western-style laws and government in the postwar era, one of the favorite pastimes of Palauans became property-rights litigation. More lawsuits involving real estate have been filed in Palau than the total number of resident citizens.

Palau is still a richly beautiful place with many fine people, but it has many problems that did not exist before the development of a tourist economy and dependence on foreign aid. Decadence and squalor have found their way into that paradise.

My hope for Basa is that it will follow a different path.

I did not make a commitment to aiding Himalayan villages to make them more like us, but neither did I want to romanticize the primitive and try to preserve Basa as I first experienced it. Carl was right that there is a temptation to want to turn Basa into a museum. That would certainly be another form of exploitation.

When I asked myself after the disaster on Mera Peak in 1999, "What the hell are we doing here?" I didn't have an answer. When I came back to Nepal in 2003 to research the changes in Sherpa culture in the fifty years since the first summit of Mount Everest, and I trekked with the Hillary family, I began to formulate an answer.

Sir Edmund Hillary partnered with Tenzing Norgay to summit Chomolungma in 1953. His philanthropic efforts with the Sherpa people over the next fifty years were also a partnership. It was not his intention to convert the Sherpas' economy from yak-herding to tourism. It was his intention to bring them the benefits of Western education and medical care, so he raised money to build schools and medical facilities in the Khumbu. As a consequence, Shepas have a higher level of education than most Nepalese and their life expectancy has increased by ten years. Hillary's family also created a trekking-tourist company and helped turn the Khumbu into an adventure-travel destination. So it goes.

The West has a lot to give developing nations. But can we bring antibiotics without bringing McDonalds and Nirvana t-shirts? During the Colonial Era, the West brought the sword of conquest and imposed Christianity on "less developed" people. In the 20th century we spread the infection of wasteful consumerism into "undeveloped" lands. In the 21st century, we need to try to get the relationship right and work in enlightened partnership across cultures.

Basa does not have the means to make improvements to its infrastructure, such as developing electricity and providing computers for the school. It does have people with tremendous strength and self-sufficiency. And the Basa villagers have been quite willing to do all the work themselves to build and renovate the school building, as well as to provide trained teachers from its own people. The challenge is to partner without fostering dependence. We can offer improvements through Western science, technology, and know-how without exploitation. And we, in turn, can receive the villagers' wisdom about how to live in communal harmony and closer to the rhythms of nature.

◙ ▤ ◎ ◙ ▤

The conversation at Niru's dinner party wound down. We were taking our last nibbles of cake and rice pudding and final sips of rakshi and beer when Ganesh said something that turned on brightly a light that had been flickering dimly in my brain since talking with Sanga on the trail by Sombare. Ganesh said that the real problem for Basa was that the farms of many of the families were not big enough to provide food for the family for the entire year. He said the farms used to provide enough, but now people lived longer and had more kids, and so the people had to find ways to make money to buy food several months each year.

I turned to Niru and asked if that was correct. He said, "Oh, yes, that is the biggest problem. The people cannot grow enough food, and the young people have to leave. Some come to Katmandu, but they do not find the jobs."

Our van driver was waiting and the others were leaving, but it was striking that Ganesh and Niru had repeated what Sanga had mentioned on the trail as "the biggest problem" for Basa. So this was what we should try to figure out. Could we—Niru, me, the people of Basa, and friends who would like to help—together solve Basa's biggest problem?

During the years that followed my Jubilee experience at the highest party in the world, I got involved with development projects for remote villages and organized trekking groups. I was developing an answer to my question in 1999 about what I was doing in Nepal. When I agreed to lead the Basa School Project and then I visited Basa, I was sure I had found my answer. It was an equation with two sides: a) help the local economy immediately through jobs with Adventure GeoTreks and help raise funds for improvements to the village requested by the village and to be carried out by the village; and b) introduce friends to Basa so they would benefit from learning about the Rai way of life.

The answer is not to make Himalayan mountain people more like Westerners. The answer is: to share. I want to share our ways with friends in Nepal, and to let them choose what they want to do with what they learn from us. And I want to facilitate friends from the West learning the ways of Nepal and of Himalayan villages. I want to help members of my groups receive from the Nepalese people what the local people want to share with us. Each person who visits Basa through a trek Niru and I plan, or who learns about its ways through participation in a project Niru and I develop, will gain from a connection with the admirable people who live in Basa. It is my hope that through the partnership Niru and I have developed we will bring our different peoples together in an exchange that will benefit Basa and its friends from the West. The exchange of sharing has transformative possibilities for both groups on economic, spiritual, and cultural levels.

This is my hope for what will grow out of my partnership with Niru. Those of us who experienced the magnetism of Basa felt the power of sharing. We shared our wealth to provide a better educational experience for the children. What Basa gave us was love. It closed a circle for me.

EPILOGUE

2009 was a painful year in several ways for me and many others. Financial pressures and a shrinking economy forced the closure of our law offices on January 1. In mid February, I tore the anterior cruciate ligament in my left knee playing volleyball and had to have replacement surgery in late April. I have been plagued by chronic neck pain and neuropathy in my right shoulder. My planned return to Nepal in October 2009 was in jeopardy.

But 2009 also included great good fortune. The Basa School Project was a success. Niru emailed photos to the donors showing the progress of the work. At the end of summer 2009, Niru reported that the 4th and 5th grade teachers had been hired, the renovation of the school building finished, the playground leveled, and a safety wall built, along with additional benches for students. All of the work was performed by Basa villagers and the two new teachers are women from the village. The instructional manuals and workbooks for all the students were shipped from Indiana to Katmandu and then delivered by air to Lukla. Porters carried the school supplies from Lukla to Basa. The compost toilet, precious to my Western sensitivities, was purchased (but not yet installed). Enough money remains in the school's trust account to pay two teachers' salaries for three years, including modest salary increases each year.

Recruiting for a 2009 expedition turned out even better than Niru and I expected. I wanted to visit Basa to see with my own eyes the improvements to the school building. Niru and I created

School floor being repaired (photo by Niru Rai)

the itinerary for a fourteen-day trek through Solu with two days in Basa and then up into the Khumbu.

My cousin David's wife, Melissa, who is blind, was so moved by David's and my descriptions of our experiences in Nepal in 2008 that she also wanted to experience it. Niru designed a tour for her to travel throughout Nepal by van and domestic flights to the lakes of Pokhara, the jungle in the Terai, and around the Katmandu Valley. My eighty-year old friend Joan, who trekked to base camp thirty years ago, and David did the tour with Melissa. David had originally planned to do the trek to Basa, as he very much wanted to experience what he missed in 2008 due to his injury on the trail, but decided just before departure that he would do the tour with Melissa and Joan instead.

Dr. John, who had signed up for the 2008 trek to Basa but broke his ribs in an auto accident a few weeks before our departure, made the trek to Basa in 2009. Two other doctor friends of John's joined up, but one had to cancel for family reasons just before departure.

Two young guys who just graduated from college were in the group. It was especially rewarding to introduce the next generation of Americans to the majesty of the Himalayas, the wonders of Nepal, and the magnetism of Basa.

All sixteen members of the 2009 trekking group made it to Basa. We brought additional supplies for the school, and small stuffed animals and glider planes for the children. Two members brought letters from grade school classes in American schools and helped to establish pen pal relationships between the American and Basa school children. Several members pledged to help form a core of fundraising volunteers for the hydroelectric project to fulfill Niru's dream to bring electricity to Basa.

Niru's vision for his home village is coming to fruition. Surveys have been completed for the hydroelectric project and fund raising is to begin in May 2010. Indianapolis First Friends Quaker Meeting has agreed to serve as the fiscal agent for the hydroelectric project, and our plan is to purchase computers and Internet service for the school as well. We have calculated that for $20,000, all seventy-five homes around the village can receive electricity from generators to be installed in a nearby river, and computers and Internet access can be provided for each classroom. Through the Internet, the school children will be able to connect with friends of the school more directly. The first step of realizing Carl's vision of Basa's children leapfrogging from medieval agriculture to the 21st century may be taken in the autumn of 2010.

Mike Miller, a retired electrical engineer who has a keen interest in Nepal and philanthropy, has consulted with us. He plans to join me for a return to Basa in the fall of 2010 to help complete the hydroelectric project. A friend's family foundation is studying the possibility of providing smokeless stoves to the village, and Niru has had a demo stove installed in his Basa home so that Mike and I may report back to the foundation about its effectiveness.

Each family will have to pay a monthly user fee for electricity, and the village will be responsible for maintaining the system. Villagers will provide the labor for installing the generators and lines, which will be purchased from and supervised by a Katmandu company. The school board will be responsible for maintaining the school's computers and paying Internet service fees. If smokeless stoves are to be provided to the village, the plan is that each family will pay a portion of the cost up to the full amount, depending on finanacial ability.

Niru, Ganesh, Sanga, and I have agreed through email correspondence that we should try to solve "the biggest problem," which is the inability of many Basa family farms to support the entire family, thus forcing young people to the cities only to find that there are no jobs there for poor and uneducated farm kids. But we don't have a plan yet. We've corresponded about family planning, and perhaps we can find a way to help make farming more efficient. I am looking forward to spending up to five days in Basa in 2010 to meet with villagers and better learn their understanding of "the biggest problem." Perhaps I can help figure out a solution to this problem, but the solution must be agreed upon by the village, and it must be their solution to implement.

I still have a sense of tragic apprehension about the future of Basa. Was it right to bring a group of sixteen trekkers to the idyllic village? How many groups of Westerners will it take before the wonderful welcome Carl, Karen, and I received transmogrifies into programmed theater for the tourists? What can be done to try to ensure that increasing contact with Westerners and modernity create a positive exchange for Basa, as well as the visitors?

Our welcome by the village was as amazing in 2009 as it was in 2008. But a member of our group did engage in the first commercial transaction with a villager by buying an antique knife. Is this the first step down the path toward developing a consumer economy? Like the Khumbu Sherpas, it is understandable that the residents of Basa want electricity, plumbing, and a money-based economy supported by tourism. To paraphrase Ang Temba Sherpa: "You wouldn't want to walk a mile to fetch water if running water can be piped into your house. Why should we?" Indeed, why should they?

But many Sherpas may only have seen what they would gain in comfort and material wealth—not what would be lost in community. And the Rai of Basa Valley will not have the compensation of gaining fame as the greatest mountain climbers in the world, as the Sherpas did. If the idyllic community, which has sustained itself as is for hundreds of years, becomes a tourist destination, will it lose its love of flower gardens? Will its people turn to drinking rakshi out of sadness over lost ways, like the Palauans? These are dark thoughts.

I have seen other villages—in the Khumbu, Pacific Island nations such as Palau, Tonga, and French Polynesia, and Latin America, for that matter—that traded their self-sufficiency for commercial tourism and a culture of dependence, to the community's detriment. Proud community reliance on the traditional economy of farming, herding, or fishing was replaced with menial, low-wage service jobs. Villages integrated with the aesthetics and rhythms of nature were despoiled by the squalor and filth of Third World urbanism.

A Third World "success" story with which I'm familiar is the transformation of a sleepy Mayan village at the ass-end of the Yucatan into the splendiferous resort of Cancun. But ride the bus to the end of the line across the causeway to see how the local Mayans who perform the low end service jobs actually live. They still exist at the bottom of the economic ladder while the government and ambitious outsiders are reaping the rewards from the commercial development.

I am not Teiresius; I don't want to be the dark prophet of doom for the beautiful delicate flower of Basa. Perhaps Basa is not so delicate and weak. With leaders like Niru, Ganesh, Sanga, and Nanda, the community may find its own path to an even more beautiful and soulful future. That is Niru's vision.

The future is not fixed. The wheel of life might turn a different direction for Basa than it has for other communities ruptured by commercial development.

I have made a commitment, and I will try to keep it. I will go forward in faith that, by saying yes to Niru, good will be served and Basa will not lose its beauty. So far in my relationship with Niru, he has shown himself to be a leader who has wisdom and compassion for the community as well as a vision for its future. I trust him.

I hold onto the hope that a meaningful exchange has taken place between the village and its friends from the West. My hope is that the exchange will lead to a deeper understanding and care for other people on the part of my trekking companions and that the friends of Basa from the West will help the village realize its dream of a good life for its children.

My prayer is that the unique power of Basa that Karen called magnetism will be strong enough to bring out enlightened generosity in my friends who visit the village, and strong enough to continue to hold its own people in its warm embrace.

*Donations to the Basa village project for hydroelectricity
and computers may be made by contacting
Jeff Rasley at jrasley@juno.com or by sending
checks to Indianapolis First Friends (Quaker Church),
3030 Kessler Blvd. E. Dr., Indianapolis, IN 46220 with
"First Friends Basa Village Project" noted as payee.*

ABOUT THE AUTHOR

Jeff Rasley is a dad and husband living in Indiana, where he practiced law for 30 years. He has been trekking and leading treks to Nepal and the Himalayas for fifteen years. Jeff has been working with the Rai people of Basa, Nepal to bring "progress" to their village in the most culturally respectful way possible. This year he will help them with a project to bring hydroelectricity to the village and computers and the Internet to the village school. He is currently raising funds for the First Friends Basa Project.

TO OUR READERS

Conari Press, an imprint of Red Wheel/Weiser, publishes books on topics ranging from spirituality, personal growth, and relationships to women's issues, parenting, and social issues. Our mission is to publish quality books that will make a difference in people's lives—how we feel about ourselves and how we relate to one another. We value integrity, compassion, and receptivity, both in the books we publish and in the way we do business.

Our readers are our most important resources, and we value your input, suggestions, and ideas about what you would like to see published. Please feel free to contact us, to request our latest book catalog, or to be added to our mailing list.

Conari Press
An imprint of Red Wheel/Weiser, LLC
500 Third Street, Suite 230
San Francisco, CA 94107
www.redwheelweiser.com